The **A** to **Z** of feelings

The
A to Z
of feelings

Making your
emotions work for you,
not against you!

ANDREW FULLER

WITH SAM FULLER

amba
press

In 2017, ABC Radio National broadcast a program called 'Three Men and a Feeling' that was based on the earliest draft of this book. My friends and compatriots on that program, Michael Mackenzie and John Hendy, deserve deep accolades and gratitude for contributing their spirited ideas to many of the feelings covered in this book.

First published in 2021 in Australia and New Zealand by Bad Apple Press, Australia. Published in 2025 by Amba Press, Melbourne, Australia
www.ambapress.com.au

Cover design and illustration: The Brewster Project
Internal design: Amba Press
Editor: Samantha Miles
Editorial assistance: Megan English

ISBN: 9781923215528 Print
ISBN: 9781923215535 eBook

A catalogue record for this book is available from the National Library of Australia.

Disclaimer: While every care has been taken in researching and compiling the information in this book, it is in no way intended to replace professional advice and counselling. Readers are encouraged to seek such help as they deem necessary. The author and publisher specifically disclaim any liability arising from the application of information in this book.

Dedicated to
Peter O'Connor and Brian Clark

About the author

Andrew Fuller is a clinical psychologist and family therapist who specialises in resilience, brains, and learning strengths. Andrew works with schools, students, and parents across the world.

Andrew is an author of many books, including: *Guerrilla Tactics for Teachers: The Essential Classroom Management Guide*, *Neuro-developmental Differentiation: Optimising Brain Systems for Learning*, *Your Best Life at Any Age*, *Tricky Kids*, *Tricky People*, *Tricky Teens*, *Unlocking Your Child's Genius*, *Raising Real People*, *From Surviving to Thriving*, *Work Smarter Not Harder* and *Beating Bullies*.

Contents

Introduction

Life is not only stranger than we imagine; it is stranger than we could ever begin to imagine. One of the greatest mysteries facing people is their own feelings: where they come from; what to do with them when they arrive; how long to let them stay and how to farewell them. Understanding our feelings is the way to stay sane in a crazy world. Knowing what our feelings mean and how to manage them can set us on a trajectory towards mental health rather than mental illness.

Understanding our feelings is also important on a global scale. We live in a world of objectification, dehumanisation and mechanisation. There is little time given for reflection and to understand the rich world of feelings. This is knowledge for which the heart is hungry.

Our external and internal worlds

When the external world is unsettling, we need access to a calm inner world. In times when shifting priorities and shifty ethics are trickling down from the very highest ranks of leadership into everyday behaviour, being aware of our inner world is the surest pathway to keeping our equilibrium.

Our bodies have six main senses: touch, smell, taste, sight, hearing and haptic (the perception of your physical self in space, which allows you to catch a ball or drive a car). These senses give us access to the external world.

Being aware of the external world helps us survive. However, if we allow our outer senses to dominate, we tend to focus more on understanding others and less on learning about ourselves. And not understanding ourselves can cost us greatly.

We also have inner senses that help us access our private world. These are our emotions and feelings. They are the inner signposts we use to learn firstly about ourselves and then others.

Most people don't know very much about their inner senses and it often shows in their relationship with themselves and other people. If you are out of tune with yourself, it is very hard to be in tune with others.

Just as we learn to develop our physical senses, we can learn to refine our inner senses and convert these into knowledge. By developing our inner senses, we make ourselves fit for creating great relationships, which is one of the basic requirements necessary for coping with all the pressures of our external world.

By the way, there is a reason why we are referring to feelings and emotions as two separate things: because they are! In the world of psychology, emotions are considered universal experiences shared by everyone, while the term 'feelings' applies to a wider range of perceptions and sensations that most, but not all, people have.

Why feelings are like a dinner party with random guests

Feelings are like unexpected dinner guests: some of them are welcome; some are picky eaters and hard to please; some don't stay long enough while others stay well beyond their use-by-date. Some become too rowdy and won't settle down while others are hard to engage, amuse and entertain.

One problem we all face is that these random dinner guests can show up without much notice and we don't have the faintest idea what to do with them. Another problem is that we tend to accept the condition of every guest as they arrive as a true reflection of reality.

To make things worse, these guests often show up in the weirdest combinations, creating mixed feelings. Having mixed feelings is a bit like watching your worst enemy drive your brand new car over a cliff.

Feelings are knowledge

'Ordinarily we do not discover the wisdom of our feelings
because we do not let them complete their work; we try to
suppress them or discharge them in premature action,
not realising that they are a process of creation which,
like birth, begins as a pain and turns into a child.'

– Alan Watts

Feelings are our deepest and earliest language. Before our ancestors had words, they survived by being astute readers of the feelings of others. Feelings communicate faster than words. Flocks of flamingos can placidly graze at a swamp but if one senses danger, in a flash they all fly off. The contagion of human feelings can be just as instantaneous.

Our feelings range from love to pain. Along the way they can pass through fear, inertia, grief, dread, anxiety, anger, shame, hatred, and the complexities of love, such as desire, lust, jealousy, need, compassion, sympathy and obsession. There has been a long history of trying to understand the perplexing inner world of feelings and emotions. Philosophers such as Plato, Plutarch, the Stoics, Thomas Aquinas, Charles Darwin, Descartes, Spinoza and Hume all wrote treatises on the various emotions. Western theologians, too, as seen in numerous religious writings, have also been concerned about what to do about feelings and emotions.

The meaning of different feelings is not always easy to read in ourselves and especially in others. Understanding the feelings of others incorrectly causes strife. Mixed signals result in relationship disputes, conflicts and misunderstandings. Misreading the signals of our own feelings causes us unnecessary suffering. At times, many of us resemble the child who becomes agitated when they need some food, not realising that hunger is the real source of their irritation. Understanding our own feelings and those of others is one of the most complex puzzles we have as humans.

The power of feelings

Feelings are our great leveller. We all have them. We can all fall victim to rages, become distressed by worries and anxieties, be consumed with jealousies and envy or berate ourselves with shame and embarrassment.

Our feelings and emotions can cause us to weep and laugh, to love and hate. They are our shared humanity. Both the richest, most famous person on the planet and the poorest share similar sets of emotions.

Feelings come from our collective ancestral experience and they all serve important purposes. There is no such thing as 'negative' feelings. The actions that result from a feeling can be negative but all feelings are valid.

The dynamic range of feelings differs between people. Some people experience the highs and lows of their feelings with operatic intensity while others putt-putt their way through life. Some motor along mildly and mostly merrily before unleashing a pyrotechnic storm of emotions that unsettles even themselves.

Broadly speaking, we can categorise many people as either 'maximisers' who express their feelings with great intensity or 'minimisers' who play down or diminish their feelings. It is likely that maximisers who read this will either emphatically declare, 'This book is amazing!' or 'This book is a *complete* waste of time.' Minimisers are more likely to comment, 'It's all right. I knew most of that before.' One thing you do need to be aware of is that maximisers and minimisers tend to marry each other.

One thing you do need to be aware of is that maximisers and minimisers tend to marry each other.

Emotions are not a luxury and they have a power that should not be underestimated. An urge arises, a passion strikes, a mood descends, feelings come over us. The way we speak of emotions is that they are active, moving, shifting forces. They often ricochet around and control our lives. We describe them as if they are external forces that possess us, although they can also be our own internal creations. They can be our guardian angels or our tormentors, acting as either a soothing balm or internal terrorists declaring war on our sense of confidence.

Emotions are detectable in specific parts of our brain but are much more than just brain activation. They are so intertwined with the experience of being human that they feature in our mythology.

Feelings are sensory and physical as much as they are emotional. Fear increases our skin conductance: surprise causes a sharp inhale of breath, embarrassment the blush of a face, disgust a visceral churning in our stomachs. Sadness and anxiety can alter sexual desire and cause fluctuations in our hormone levels. Grief can depress the immune system. Matters of the heart matter to the heart.

Our feelings rumble up from our biology to enter into our awareness, often catching us off guard. All too often we find ourselves scratching our heads and thinking, 'Why am I feeling that?' One of the most perplexing things to realise, as Lisa Feldman Barratt points out in her book *How Emotions Are Made*, is that feelings aren't things that happen to us; feelings are things that are made by us. They are built, rather than built in. We create them and base them on our physical sensations and our neuroceptions (our subconscious ability to detect threats).

Cognitive behavioural theorists originally believed our thoughts were the primary source of our feelings and, as a consequence, much of their therapy system was focused on changing thinking patterns.

However, it is now clear that feelings have multiple origins. Some begin as sensations in our body. Others start in our tingling 'spider senses' or neuroception lurking on the edges of our awareness. Others, of course, begin with an idea or thought. The more we can appreciate that there are multiple pathways for feelings to arise, the more we can differentiate between them and the better we can understand ourselves.

Feelings are attention-seeking. They sharpen our awareness. When we try to dampen them or divert them they find different ways to express themselves.

Emotions and feelings are signals from our inner senses. They are signposts we can use to guide us towards what we really need. Feelings convey a truth.

However, just because feelings are attention-grabbing does not mean that we should fall victim to their quirks and inconsiderate habits. Just as we are more than one particular thought, we are also more than one feeling. Yet many people do not pause to read or analyse their feelings. They lead lives driven by their most current emotion. This almost inevitably does not work out well, because while emotions also contain truths, they should not always be trusted. Some should be discarded. Others deserve to be interrogated. A few should be taken out the back and given a stern talking to.

How feelings can help you to read minds (even your own)

Learning to read the signposts of your own emotional world is massively advantageous. It is a secret roadmap to creating and maintaining healthy relationships with ourselves and others. Some people try to ignore their feelings, usually to their peril. It is like they are sending important messages to themselves that they never bother to open.

Knowing how to read feelings is akin to learning a second language. Learning the language of feelings is like delving into the past and recapturing a language your distant ancestors used, one that was then supplanted by a deluge of words. As mentioned previously, our distant ancestors were much better readers of micro-expressions and feelings than modern people. In the absence of words they relied on the communication of feelings to survive. Today we prefer words, which makes us over-reliant on what people say (and less on what they do). But the language of feelings is just as relevant today and will give you insights into other people and, at times, will startle you about yourself.

Would it be to your advantage if you could:

- differentiate genuine people from those who are fake?
- know who truly desires you?
- separate honest people from liars?
- know who to trust and who not to trust?
- learn from your experiences by looking inwards as well as outwards?

Do you also think it could be useful to know:

- what upsets you and what to do about it?
- how to shelve, settle and calm worries?
- how to replicate times of happiness, inspiration and creativity?
- how to react more positively to moments of anger or conflict?

Being able to read the language of feelings enables you to comprehend the complexities of day-to-day life.

What feelings can tell us

You might think that tuning yourself into the language of feelings involves reading subtle cues with all the skill and finesse of Sherlock Holmes, but it is actually fairly easy to learn. Most feelings don't whisper quietly; they scream their presence loudly.

Possessing this knowledge can help you to read others but even more importantly, it can help you to know yourself. Reading others is good but if you have no idea about what you want, what settles or upsets you, you can't steer the course of your life.

Feelings are signals, so it is worth thinking about what they are pointing out. Our world seems to value action more highly than reflection or consideration and, in doing so, denies people the ability to self-rescue. This is why thinking about your feelings and what they might mean is like having a secret super-power.

One helpful question we can ask is: What does this feeling want for us? What is it seeking?

Feeling	What it might be showing you
Anger	What you care about as well as what you believe needs to change.
Bitterness	Where you need to heal from loss.
Boasting	May indicate disappointment about not being appreciated by others or discontentment about your own life.
Disappointment	Shows you still care.
Discomfort	You need to pay attention to what is happening. It is often an invitation to change.
Envy and jealousy	It is time to love and look after yourself more.
Grief	The love you have for someone or something you have lost keeps them alive in your heart.

Feeling	What it might be showing you
Guilt	You are still living by other people's expectations of who you should be.
Resentment	Shows where you are living in the past.
Sadness and heartbreak	The depth of your care for others and the world.
Shame	You need to start living up to your own values, rather than trying to be someone other people expect you to be.
Vulnerability	Shows you are brave enough to be you.

Just pausing and saying to yourself, 'I am having this feeling. I wonder what that is about and what it is wanting?' gives you a lag time between your feelings and your actions. Considering your feelings and what they might mean can lessen the powerful grip they have on your life. Sometimes, pausing and noticing can save your life. This is true in potentially violent circumstances and it can also save you from misplacing your trust in people who will betray you.

It's more than a feeling

Our feelings and emotions affect even the most fleeting parts of our lives. Some emotions we pursue and long for. Others chase us like the hounds of hell. Some are placid and barely noticeable; others are untamed beasts.

The reductionist may simplify our feelings to hormones and neurotransmitters. Love could be reduced to oxytocin, our own personal hormonal love potion. Fear can be sited in the amygdala. Ruminative despair can be viewed as an over-activity in the pre-frontal cortex. None of these explanations, however, fully explain the true human resonance of love, or the extent of dread, or the bleakness of enduring loss and sadness.

There is a powerful poetry to feelings that can't be boiled down to simplistic explanations. The purpose of science is not to cure us of a sense of mystery; it is to reinvent and reimagine mystery. Consequently, this book draws upon many sources to help us understand feelings: philosophy, song, poetry, psychology, literature, myth, biology, spirituality and antiquity.

Clearly, some of our feelings have triggers that are buried in instinct. Some of our feelings are so ingrained in our ancestral past they communicate more clearly and powerfully than words ever could. People are innately fearful of spiders, vomiting, snakes, the dark and certain sounds such as growling.

Interpreting feelings helps reveal general rules of thumb about people and their lives. This helps us to form a basis on which to forge healthy connections and relationships.

Mind reading for beginners

Improving our understanding of feelings and how people relate to them deepens our capacity to interpret the world and respond to it effectively.

Some rules of thumb

- We all seek some connection with others.
- We seek to be loved and love others.
- We are saddened by loss and try to avoid it.
- We dislike rejection.
- We are often unduly harsh about people who we once loved but feel let us down.
- We like recognition and attention.
- We will do more to avoid pain than we will to seek pleasure.
- We acutely dislike ridicule and embarrassment.
- We care what others think of us.
- We seek a degree of control in our lives.
- When there are three people, two will often gang up on the other one.
- We often divide the world into 'us' and 'them'.
- We generally like people who are like us but we have to differentiate from people who are too much like us.
- We seek to feel superior to someone else.

Feelings are healthiest when they flow: E-motion

From our first sharp intake of breath after our birth to our last sighing outbreath, we are beset with feelings.

If we have no understanding of our emotions, we become the victim of our most current feeling, whether that is joy, rage, envy or anxiety.

Apart from our first intake of breath and our final last sigh, every breath we have comes in a pair. We breathe in and we breathe out. Just as our breath has a cycle of in and out, our feelings have a gathering in and a letting go. The in and the out is the natural process of life. Feelings come and go. This is the secret beauty that is contained within the word emotion. It accurately describes what we need to do – keep our feelings in motion.

Life is change and movement. To stay emotionally balanced, we need to be aware of our feelings shifting. When we function well, we view our emotions as transitory passing processes rather than permanent moods. When we see a feeling as being permanent, we become transfixed by it and get stuck.

One way of thinking about mental ill health is that it occurs when feelings become stuck. We become like hamsters running on a treadmill: lots of effort but going nowhere fast. An example is when people are stricken with anxieties or devastated by recurrent sadness or grief. Often they have the same thoughts and feelings over and over again. Good mental health is the capacity to allow feelings to occur and to then flow through us.

In a personal sense, understanding your feelings helps you to get some perspective on your life and what you want to do with it. Knowing this could change the course of your life. It helps you create your life, rather than just react to your feelings.

One of the easiest ways to change your life is to alter the way you think. Your thoughts are driven by what you notice. What you notice is often driven by your feelings. We often feel before we think. By noticing and reflecting on your feelings, you free yourself to think differently.

A note for readers

This is not a book to read from start to finish. It is a book to dip in and out of as feelings arise. There are appendices at the back of the book that will help you to identify some of the most common feelings, and the most likely physical signs that accompany each feeling.

The next section describes a series of feelings arranged in alphabetical order. Consider it a recipe book for feelings! You wouldn't read the whole recipe book if you were just looking for a quick dessert; you are more likely to just consult the section relevant to you at the time.

Each feeling has four main sections.

1. A description of common states that accompany the feeling.
    The words above the line describe what is happening on the outside or the feelings portrayed to the external world. The words below the line describe the inner experience of the feeling.

Kindness, Self-compassion, Self-worth, Creativity, Playfulness, Acknowledgement

Confidence, Tolerance, Openness, Freedom, Flexibility, Understanding, Integration

2. What you may notice when the feeling occurs.
3. What happens at the time of the feeling.
4. What you can do to help the feeling work for you, not against you.

Throughout this book we will also discuss, where possible, the likely relationship between our feelings and what is going on in the brain. The risk of doing this, however, is that it can give the false impression that brain function causes feelings. It is not so simple.

As I have mentioned before, many feelings don't have their origins in the brain at all. Many begin as a vague form of body awareness called neuroceptions. These are the hunches, the vibes or the sense that something shonky might be going on. This all happens quicker than you can notice. One common pattern is:

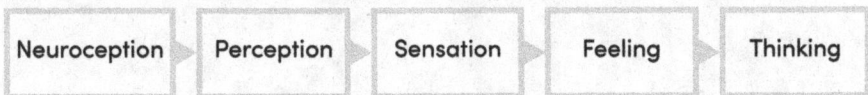

| Neuroception | Perception | Sensation | Feeling | Thinking |

However, trying to put a linear sequence into the world of feelings is destined to be wrong. The beauty of our feelings is their refusal to be completely explained by simple answers. They are complex and that is what gives life its richness.

Your body is an intricate information processing system with each part affecting others. This means that while some feelings will start as body senses that convert into feelings and thoughts, other feelings begin as thoughts, some of which can then create major effects in the body.

While this area of research is emerging and developing, one thing is clear: we are often trying to cope with feelings that are dealing with the complexities of a modern world with a brain that uses design principles laid down one or two million years ago.

Acceptance

Kindness, Self-compassion, Self-worth, Creativity, Playfulness, Acknowledgement

Confidence, Tolerance, Openness, Freedom, Flexibility, Understanding, Integration

'When I accept myself just as I am, then I can change.'

– Carl R Rogers

What you may notice

Acceptance is about becoming less reliant on praise, feedback and affirmations from others and, instead, being kinder to yourself. It is related to confidence and a sense of assuredness, and opens up the way towards creating your own path.

Acceptance is not passivity. Acceptance can appear less dynamic than setting goals and making plans for self-improvement. As we will see with many of the feelings covered in this book, it is easy to be discontented. It is easier to be, as PG Wodehouse superbly put it, if not quite disgruntled, not entirely gruntled either.

It is far easier to squander energies trying to resolve discontentment. It takes real consideration and careful action to be contented.

Acceptance is a form of alignment that shifts us towards contentment. When we lack self-acceptance we can view ourselves as needing changing and improvement. There is a sense of not quite being in control of the direction of our life.

The world tricks people into feeling dissatisfied with their current state of being. 'You are not good enough' is the main message. Consumerism relies upon it. The question the world seems to attack people with is, 'Why accept who you are now when you could be fitter/thinner/happier/richer/smarter/even more successful?' Diet harder, exercise harder, work longer or rush faster are messages that place people on the treadmill of self-improvement. Invariably, this is accompanied by offers to sell you some product to help you achieve your new, improved state of being.

Self-acceptance takes patience. It is a type of alchemy that we do on ourselves. There are parts of ourselves that we find admirable and easy to like. There are other parts that we regard as distasteful and a little, well … grubby. (Don't worry, we're just talking about people in general here. I'm sure this doesn't apply to you!) However, our flaws are just as important as our more positive qualities.

Our flaws are just as important as our more positive qualities.

Self-acceptance is about making the best of the bits we like while acknowledging the bits we're not so fond of and channelling them in positive directions. For example, someone who tends to be controlling can use this to become a meticulous, detail-orientated person and possibly seek a career as an events or project manager.

Often the journey towards self-acceptance begins with being accepted by loved ones. We first glimpse ourselves reflected in the eyes of those we love.

While change is always possible, without awareness, reflection and some degree of self-acceptance, most attempts are dashed by disappointment, followed by self-loathing. This sets up an unhappy cycle of failed efforts.

Acceptance is awareness rather than passivity. It doesn't mean we have to be resigned or content with situations as they are. Accepting that this is how things are for now leads us to a sense of awareness and being present. Becoming aware and being present opens us up to new possibilities.

Self-acceptance is a pathway to recovery and healing. Life transitions such as relationship breakups, job changes, health changes or fluctuations in fortunes can jolt us all. Through self-acceptance people begin to learn that they are larger than their damaging misfortunes. At these times, self-acceptance restores trust in yourself, which enables you to move beyond periods of hurt and tough times.

Without self-acceptance we can be tempted to try to conceal parts of ourselves at a cost to our integrity. Self-acceptance empowers us to be authentic.

What happens

One of the central longings of people is to be acknowledged, to be accepted for who they are. When we feel accepted there is a sense of calm belonging. We don't have to be on guard or defend ourselves. We can speak more freely, think more creatively and live more playfully.

True acceptance of others requires acceptance of ourselves. We have to be brave enough to celebrate the parts of our own self that we like and courageous enough to look those parts that we aren't so fond of in the eye and admit they also are part of who we are.

It can be an act of great liberation to re-label some of our most troubling flaws as treasures.

Without acceptance, those disliked aspects of ourselves seem to clamour their way into our lives anyway. The parts of ourselves that we don't find acceptable we tend to find infuriating in other people. Sigmund Freud called this projection – we take the parts of ourselves that we don't like, notice them in other people and then blame them for it.

What you can do that helps

Some people think self-acceptance is about knowing yourself so well there is an inner clarity and harmony, as if thoughts, feelings, behaviours and intentions are all aligned. However, we are more complex and more contradictory than that. While unity of acceptance may wonderful, it is rare. Acceptance is not simplifying yourself down to one understanding.

There is a labyrinth inside everyone, and a diversity of selves. Sometimes the selves work together, sometimes they contradict and conflict with one another. See the box below for examples.

I want to be carefree.	I want to be successful.
I want freedom.	I want a secure relationship.
I want to be a team player.	I want to be a winner.
I want to do good in the world.	I want a nice car, house.
I want to be kind.	I can be greedy.

It is easy to dismiss our contradictions as irrational. But this non-acceptance of the richness of ourselves robs us of vital understanding.

Contradictions are actually complexities and possibilities jostling with one another. Real acceptance is about being aware of the different aspects of yourself and letting them communicate with one another.

There are times in most people's lives when the different aspects of ourselves don't get along. Different demands or desires compete for space inside our heads and we feel stuck and confused. These are conundrums we need to wrestle with, aiming not for one side to submit, but for both to merely talk to each other.

One way to get through contradictions like this is to complete a process called inner work, as outlined by Robert Johnson. Essentially, this involves starting a journal where you write a conversation between the different points of view, wishes, demands or desires.

Example:

Self 1:   I should move to the country.

Self 2:   But you love shops and shows!

Self 1:   Yes, but I also love gardens and animals.

Self 2:   Cities have gardens and there are always zoos and farm stays.

The point of this is not to have one part or the other dominate or try to convince the other but just simply to have the different parts of you communicate without needing to come to an instant resolution.

You may write the different parts using different pens or use upper and lower case. Write only until you feel you have expressed the inner turmoil of your thoughts and impulses and then stop. When the feelings bubble up again, open up the journal and continue the conversation.

It may take some time but gradually a resolution will emerge. It is best that you don't rush it. Often it takes about six weeks for people to clearly realise what it is they really want to do.

Welcome what is

These three words convey a philosophy of life.

There are two ways out of a problem: accept what's happening, see the positive, and choose a peaceful state of mind; or fight against it and be miserable.

Accepting what's happening can look like stepping back for a time from trying to alter the course of events, or temporarily giving up trying to persuade, inspire, cajole or motivate other people.

The world seems to find this idea of acceptance very challenging. The fear is that practising acceptance will make you into a compliant, docile, lotus-eating walkover. Instead, welcoming what *is* will make you more aware of others and give you greater flexibility with yourself. It will also increase your courage. Try it. Next time you meet a judgmental person, look them in the eye and ask yourself: 'What would it be like to live behind those eyes?' Acceptance is having the courage to face such questions.

Acceptance is a choice and it is a hard one, but sometimes it is the only real choice we have. It's hard to practise acceptance when you deeply wish things weren't the way they are. The truth is, we can't always change our reality, even though we try. So instead of staring at the closed door in front of us or getting tired and bruised trying to break it down, turn around and see how many other windows and doors we can open.

Acceptance does not mean that you like it, agree with it, or want it. It is simply the act of accepting it.

Physical signs of acceptance/non-acceptance

When people don't feel accepted, they can seem:

- stressed
- judged
- misunderstood
- wary
- tired for no reason and experience headaches
- irritable
- snappy or argumentative.

When people feel accepted, they seem:

- creative
- peaceful
- communicative
- calm
- connected to others.

From 'have to' to 'get to'

Acceptance lightens our hearts and deepens our connections. One way to do this is to shift ourselves from thinking 'have to' to 'get to'. We all experience 'have to' in our lives. We have to pay the bills, have to get the car serviced, have to see a dentist, have to get a check-up and so on. Stop for a moment and think about all your wonderful ancestors: people who can't do any of the things you can because they are no longer with us.

One way to practise acceptance is the next time you notice yourself doing a 'have to' (and you will because you are a human like the rest of us), stop, pause and turn it into a 'get to'.

For example, instead of saying or thinking: 'I have to visit my family,' you could say 'I get to have a family I can visit.' Rather than thinking 'I have to go to work,' you could say, 'I get to have a job and go to work.'

What's going on in the acceptance brain?

When you feel accepted, your hypothalamus and pituitary gland are releasing oxytocin, which is a hormone associated with feelings of trust, love and connection, as well as acceptance. The endorphins of pleasure surge through your body. Your stress levels lower and the amygdala (the gateway for fear and stress) quietens. Your feel-good neurotransmitters of dopamine and serotonin increase.

Addition

Devotion, Desire, Attraction, Compulsion, Obsession, Love, Yearning, Craving, Loyalty

Enslavement, Isolation, Poor self-care, Guilt, Trapped, Resentful

'Addiction: When you can give up something any time,
as long as it's next Tuesday.'

– Nikki Sixx, lead singer, Motley Crue

We are all addicted to something, whether it is alcohol, drugs, smoking, love, attention, respect, contacts, money, power, holidays, adrenaline, phones, video games, fitness, food, gambling, self-harm or even breathing, so this feeling applies to you. You name it – someone out there is probably addicted to it.

What you may notice

There is a desperate complicity to addictions. Addictions are like bad love affairs that promise ecstatic highs but result in rock-bottom lows and are incredibly hard to leave. There is a compulsive repetition to addictions (see Obsession, page 179). Often the same pattern is repeated in ritualistic detail.

At the heart of addiction is a sense of inadequacy. What drives the addiction is the idea that by supplementing the self with something, you will be complete. Our inadequacies often show themselves most vividly to us in relationships and social settings.

What happens

Every addict I have ever treated, and it must be thousands by now, has had the holy trinity of needs that underpin the addiction.

These are:

1. A degree of social anxiety or awkwardness that a person finds frightening or uncomfortable in some way and desperately wants to conceal.

2. A deletion of dopamine. Dopamine is a neurotransmitter that transmits messages between the nerves that travel around the brain and body. It is a precursor to how much happiness or pleasure we can feel in life, and to emotional regulation. Too much or too little can cause a range of health issues. In people suffering from an addiction, too little means that their daily life is less exciting and fulfilling. Initially, anxiety may be the cause of taking less pleasure in events, but as time and the addiction goes on, levels of dopamine drop further and further. As the old saying goes, the thrill is gone.

3. Loopy, repetitive behaviours. When a person finds a way to relieve their social anxiety and loss of pleasure, they tend to use the same method over and over again. Typically this involves an over-activated anterior cingulate gyrus – the part of our brain's limbic system that is involved in processing emotions and behaviour regulation. When the frontal part of our limbic system becomes overstimulated, we have 'loopy' thinking, which means we literally do the same things over and over again. The more we do it, the less dopamine is produced, which makes us want to do the behaviour even more. And so on.

The order in which these three factors occur varies from person to person but all are involved in addiction.

Usually you will either accidentally or intentionally find a method to compensate for feelings of social awkwardness and/or anxiety. This is often successful in the short term. You then might find a tribe or a social group where your interests are shared and you feel accepted. You might also feel indebted to your new social group and deeply loyal to them. However, the thrill of the addictive act soon diminishes rewards from other activities. When not involved in your addictive activity, life seems drab and mundane. This process makes it almost inevitable that your addiction will become your primary focus in life. You are either satisfying your addiction or enduring the times in between when you can't.

Just like in a passionate love affair, all other relationships, whether with friends, family or co-workers, fall by the wayside. If they are not helping you to facilitate your addiction they will be of little or no interest to you. This can lead to people in your life feeling betrayed, used or abandoned, which in turn causes you to feel guilt and shame. You can also feel powerless to rectify this.

Physical signs of addiction

- cravings
- obsession
- loss of pleasure when the addictive element is not accessible
- narrowed thinking
- loss of joy
- anticipation.

What you can do that helps

Overcoming an addiction is a process of grieving. It is like giving up a cherished love and opening yourself to the possibility of meeting someone new. Guilt, shame and grief are a powerful mix and can stop you developing the sense of self-worth that helps you to move to better ways of being. For that reason, addictions need to be altered gradually and gently. It is a slow recalibration.

Early steps involve finding places, tribes, groups and people outside your addictive activity. Connecting with people, whether through friends, family or a specialised program, is one of the most powerful first steps to take.

The sharp harshness of life without an addiction can be overwhelming if you have spent years being comfortably numb. You will feel raw and tender to the viewpoints of others. Be aware that there are many people who will want to condemn addicted people and that being exposed to too many opinions can be toxic. Be careful and selective about who you hang out with.

Also be aware that there will be ups and downs in the process of recovery and possibly times of relapse. Learning how to feel complete and worthwhile without access to an addictive substance or activity will take time. It is a process of re-learning life. Just as in grief we need to learn how to live life without someone, recovering from addiction is learning how to live life without something.

The idea of replacing one addiction with a more constructive addiction is utter rubbish. Abseiling does not adequately replace heroin. Jogging, cycling or mountain climbing does not replace the rush of using ice. It would be like saying to you, 'Your parent has passed away but I've found you a substitute one who is almost as good.' It is also difficult to find a replacement tribe to associate with comfortably.

You don't always stop being addicted but you can be helped to live without things or people that are destructive to you.

What's going on in the addicted brain?

Addictive drugs alter the reward circuits in the brain, particularly the dopamine system situated in the lower part of the brain, called the nucleus accumbens.

Some drugs release up to ten times the amount of dopamine provided by natural rewards (for example, exercise, eating chocolate) and they do it more reliably.

As your nucleus accumbens is flooded with dopamine, your hippocampus lays down memories of this rapid sense of satisfaction and the amygdala creates a conditioned response: drug use feels good.

Ambiguity

Open-minded, Curious, Puzzled, Tolerant, Open, Surprise, Shock, Worried

Bewildered, Uncertain, Doubtful, Hesitant, Dubious, Waver, Dread, Prevaricating

> *'The greater the doubt, the greater the awakening;*
> *the smaller the doubt, the smaller the awakening.*
> *No doubt, no awakening.'*
>
> – CC Chang, *The Practice of Zen*

We don't much like being uncertain or confused for long periods. We prefer answers and explanations to make sense of what's happening around us. Our dislike of uncertainty has driven invention and innovation for centuries. Uncertainty drives curiosity and, over the long term, it's served us well.

Being able to tolerate uncertainty is related to acceptance and to creativity.

What you may notice

Our relationship with ambiguity and uncertainty is complex. Over long periods we dislike it; over short periods it thrills and engages us. This is what engages us in films and stories.

Physical signs of confusion and ambiguity

- patting the back of the head
- tilting the head
- tapping the forehead with the fingertips

- arching a hand over one eye with a thumb against a cheek and the fingers against the forehead
- squinting eyes
- eyebrows not level
- looking sideways
- rubbing the back of the neck.

Uncertainty activates our threat system while the attainment of certainty rewards us with dopamine. Cycling through these stages keeps us engaged.

We can be inclined to latch onto an answer too quickly, rather than live in the uncertainty for a bit longer to see if a more suitable or interesting response is still at hand. Unknowingly, we trade possibility for certainty. But there's rarely any room for possibility in certainty.

In our workshops on personal resilience, about halfway through, some participants will usually appear fatigued and frustrated. This is the hurdle to cross or wait out, if you will. It is usually in this moment of feeling blocked or stalled that there's a fierce temptation to turn back, or to seize the nearest reasonable solution in order to make some progress.

This is when we need to be able to tolerate ambiguity and that requires relinquishing control, even though a solution isn't always guaranteed, in order to make room for new and emerging connections to crystalise into a clear direction. It also means accepting the fact that there might be numerous ways of answering the same question, each with different but potentially positive results. So how do you cultivate this tolerance for ambiguity?

What happens

Our brain craves certainty. It equates certainty with safety. Think of your brain as a prediction device. Massive neuronal resources are devoted to predicting what will happen in each moment. Your brain receives patterns from the outside world, stores them as memories, and makes predictions by combining what it has seen before with what is happening. Prediction is not just one of the things your brain does, it is the primary function of the neo-cortex and the foundation of intelligence.

We don't just hear; we hear and predict what should come next. We don't just see; we predict what we should be seeing moment to moment.

Like an addiction to anything, when the craving for certainty is met, there is a sensation of reward. At low levels, for example predicting where your foot will land as you walk, the reward is often unnoticeable (except when your foot doesn't land the way you had predicted, which equates to uncertainty and sometimes pain). The pleasure of prediction is more acute when you listen to music based on repeating patterns. The ability to predict, and then obtain data that meets those predictions, generates an overall positive response. It's part of the reason that mind games like Solitaire, Sudoku and crosswords are enjoyable. They give you a little rush from creating more certainty in the world, in a safe way. Some people prefer cleaning the house or organising their files to get the same kind of reward.

What you can do that helps

Here are a few ideas that have helped people in the past to cope with the discomfort of uncertainty.

Mind stretching

Be more interested in questions than answers. Access your inner three-year-old and ask why, why, why? Say things like, 'Tell me more about that.'

Stay aware and suspend judgment: Many people stop thinking as soon as they make a judgment. Take it all in as interesting data.

Enjoy the mess

The creative process is rarely neat and tidy. Consider this an opportunity that allows you to be messy.

Take it slow

The world that's asking for order is demanding speed as well. Often we falsely equate importance with urgency. Slow things down and take your time to look at things for longer, ask more questions than you'd normally permit yourself, and generate more ideas and options before selecting among them.

The risk in rushing towards certainty is a failure to prioritise. If we don't take the time to consider and evaluate, we can confuse what seems urgent with what is important.

Look twice

Life is more interesting if you can develop the patience to stick with uncertainty and explore possibilities. Play with questions, ideas and concepts and try them on for size. Follow threads of thought, pretending something might work, and see where it takes you. Live, temporarily, with possible options to see if they are useful or not. This is a way of enriching your life – develop the patience to stay with uncertainty and explore possibilities.

Meet your dorso-lateral pre-frontal cortex

Two parts of the frontal lobes in the brain appear to be involved in decision-making. The orbital pre-frontal cortex (OPFC) tends to like clarity and determines what the constraints or routines of a situation are and makes decisions accordingly. The OPFC may make decisions based on precedence and tradition. The dorso-lateral pre-frontal cortex (DLPFC) on the other hand tends to evaluate the pros and cons of a situation and then decide accordingly. Ideally, of course, we become adept at both ways of resolving our doubts and making decisions.

Ambition

Eager, Keen, Enthusiastic, Passionate, Driven, Desire, Go-getting, Successful

Coveting, Vainglory, Arrogant, Boastful, Maniacal, Exhaustion, Burned-out

'The best laid plans of mice and men. Will go astray.'
– Robbie Burns

To be ambitious is often viewed positively in our world. There are people who become multi-millionaires, such as entrepreneurs with start-up companies, who have rich social lives and go on to make meaningful contributions to society.

The risk is it can come at a cost. Taken too far, ambition can topple the successful person straight into Type-A, driven behaviour and heart attack territory.

Our most common reaction to achievements is not satisfaction but a craving for more.

What you may notice

Ambition can have enormous payoffs, but care needs to be taken that this feeling doesn't narrow you as a person. People who experience success early in life can be most susceptible to this. The heady sense of early success results in a single focus on that area to the exclusion of other interests. A person can flourish in their area of chosen success only to become twisted and stunted in others. It is often in midlife that these people, after they have climbed the ladder of success, sit back and realise that they placed their ladder against someone else's wall.

For those who are susceptible, ambition and pride can be their biggest weaknesses. In essence, the root of their success can also contain the seed of their downfall.

There is a saying that some people believe their own publicity. Swept up and inflated with the glories of their own successes, they believe the usual rules of society don't apply to them. They believe they have the golden touch and often think that their success in one area of life is transferrable to other areas. Quite often this ends disastrously.

Ambition left unchecked becomes hubris, which is the opposite of humility. Over-reaching ambition is a monster that can devour us. The flaws and dangers of ambition converted into hubris are conveyed in many great works of literature.

The Greek myth of Icarus tells how he and his inventor father, Daedalus, escape from the island of Crete by means of wings they have created out of bird feathers and wax. Before they set out, Daedalus gives an impassioned warning to his son to fly neither too high, in case the heat of the sun melts the wax holding the wings together, or too low, in case he falls into the sea. Icarus ignores his father's warning and soars higher and higher to the sun, before plunging headlong to his death in the sea below.

Of course, we are all flawed. Indeed, it may be our flaws that are the most lovable part of ourselves.

It may be our flaws that are the most lovable part of ourselves.

One of the salutary lessons about the dangers of undiluted ambition is the story of Scrooge in Charles Dickens's *A Christmas Carol*. While hopefully we have not been as mean and miserly as Scrooge, the story nevertheless provides us with a necessary wake-up call.

In *A Christmas Carol*, Scrooge is already in a state of living death. It is Christmas Eve and Scrooge is demonstrating his usual mean ways by rejecting his nephew's invitation to dinner, refusing to donate to a charity for the poor and threatening to dock a day's pay from his clerk, Bob Cratchitt, for not working on Christmas Day.

Scrooge is then visited by three ghosts: Christmas Past, Christmas Present and Christmas To Come. Christmas Past shows him how he transformed from a pleasant young man into a solitary monster obsessed by money. Christmas Present shows him happy families enjoying

Christmas, and Christmas Future shows him a version of himself as dead, unmourned, unloved and forgotten. Scrooge recognises it is time to construct more positive relationships and undertakes to change his behaviour.

The ambitious brain

Dopamine is the neurochemical most associated with the motivation behind ambition and pride. Dopamine affects us before we obtain rewards as it encourages us to act.

People who are hard workers often have higher dopamine levels in the striatum and pre-frontal cortex – two areas known to impact motivation and reward. Less-ambitious people have dopamine present in the anterior insula, an area of the brain involved in risk perception.

A usually level-headed person can become intoxicated by a heady rush of testosterone mixed with dopamine. This is a time when a person can become reckless and feel over-confident in their abilities.

What you can do that helps

'Nothing in excess' was written over the Temple of Apollo in Delphi. And so it goes, be wealthy but use your wealth to make a meaningful contribution to people's lives. When we stay connected to the idea that we have our own life and we can make a positive contribution to others, we tend to remain humble and grounded.

The greatest leaders are not those with the biggest egos or the greatest vision. Great leadership is more about presence than ambition. Great leaders inspire greatness in others. They are positive, take action, are likeable, proactively deal with issues as they arise and take responsibility for solving things. In this instance, ambition is not just an ego-driven quest for adulation; it fuels a desire to make a contribution for a greater good.

Different ways to be ambitious

Broadly speaking, we can think of ambitious people who are primarily ladder climbers and others who are primarily tapestry weavers. The ladder climbers find it hard to fit more than one person on each rung, so by necessity, one person needs to be higher up and more powerful than the other. Tapestry weavers like to put out threads of connection and want to sit at the centre of their weave. There are advantages and disadvantages to both ways of being.

Ladder climbers have a strong sense of justice. They often have one main mission or purpose in their lives. Usually they are more focused on themselves than on their social groups and have a few important relationships. Focused and determined, they are all set up for achievement and action and don't have a lot of time for feelings or consultation. They often value being respected over being trusted.

Tapestry weavers have almost entirely different priorities. They have multiple missions. They have their own purposes and a lot of other people's purposes as well. Tapestry weavers care for a broad range of people. Tuned into other people's lives, they may hold off accomplishing their own projects in order to make sure people are cared for.

Now before you start thinking that the ladder climbers are just a bunch of proud, heartless overachievers and the tapestry weavers are lovely, warm and fuzzy, we need to get a bit of balance here.

Ladder climbers get things done. Some, but not all, are quite happy to have other people climb ladders too. They can enjoy the beauty of the tapestry even though they may not understand why it is important that it is there.

Being at the centre of the tapestry can be more about enabling others rather than directly accomplishing things yourself. Being so tuned into everyone else can make decisive action difficult. Inclusivity can be valued over expertise. When everyone's opinion is important, prioritisation can be difficult. Who is right when everyone is right?

> **When everyone's opinion is important,**
> **prioritisation can be difficult.**
> **Who is right when everyone is right?**

Tapestry weavers might be able to appreciate what ladder climbing brings in terms of advantages and may at times be able to feign interest in the whole ladder-climbing business, but really, they aren't that much interested in climbing ladders.

They like to develop more distributed and complex relationships and link people together. Some tapestry weavers enter into a secret pact: they will sit at the centre of the weave but expect that everyone else will appreciate the sacrifice they are making by being there.

This trade-off doesn't always work out well. Watching other people shine in your own tapestry can be a bit galling. Not feeling appreciated for your contribution can lead to bitterness and feeling overlooked.

Being at the top of the ladder isolates you from the web; being at the centre of the web means you can only be halfway up the ladder. What feels safe for one is dangerous for the other.

Now, what is really interesting is creating the possibility for yourself of being both a ladder climber and a tapestry weaver.

Ambition always involves a shift in power. Power is not bad in itself but attaining it always comes at a cost. Other parts of life are usually neglected. For example, pessimists are often the possessors of power. If you are ever in a meeting and hear people object to a promising new idea or initiative, they will often be the people who fear they will lose some of their power if the idea is implemented.

Becoming aware of these feelings, the patterns and the risks involved, including pride and over-confidence, will help you to avoid some of the pitfalls this feeling can create.

Anger

Aggravation, Annoyance, Frustration, Indignation

Frustration, Irritation, Seething, Hostile, Vengeful, Fury, Rage, Wrath, Bitterness, Hurt

*'Anybody can become angry – that is easy, but to be angry with
the right person and to the right degree and at the right time and
for the right purpose, and in the right way – that is not within
everybody's power and is not easy.'*

– Aristotle

Anger is often spoken of as a hot emotion: she became enraged; he
seethed; she fumed; he flared up; they boiled over; it was a fiery meeting.
In terms of how anger is experienced, however, people roughly divide
into two groups: hot heads and cold hearts.

The hot heads explode with a pyrotechnic display of anger. Their
anger flares and flickers like an enraged dragon. The cold hearts just
quietly smoulder away before calculating the best chances of achieving
justice or revenge for past hurts and sleights.

What you may notice

Although anger is usually viewed as a 'negative' emotion, it is a very
valuable feeling because it shows we care deeply about something.
It signals what is really important to us. It helps us create personal
boundaries and know where we stand on important issues in life. It is
also a sign that we need to take care of ourselves or to protect ourselves
from something. It arises in the face of a real or even perceived threat to
our personal boundaries or core beliefs. If we miss that message, not only
might we find ourselves in harm's way, our anger can go unchecked and

become uncontrolled. Anger left unleashed can shame us. You don't have it; it has you. And projecting anger onto someone doesn't help: you risk missing what it is trying to tell you.

Anger is an outer response to an inner sense of powerlessness, and vulnerability. Deeply buried behind anger is hurt and grief. It can lurk and smoulder for a long time before erupting in a wild flash. Most things that make us angry are deeply rooted in incidents experienced in our earlier years.

Angry people live in angry bodies. Anger gives vigour to the muscles and energy to the will. It changes our voice. Mouths froth. Eyebrows go down, eyelids have an upper flare, while the lower eyelids flatten. When we give out the death glare our lips tighten, our teeth clench, and sometimes our jaw juts forwards.

If we spend too long being angry we can place ourselves at risk, physically and mentally, and make unwise life decisions. Being angry for too long is like ingesting poison. The cost comes in the heart. People with tempers and anger issues are at higher risk of heart problems. This is especially the case if we become consumed with anger and do not find ways to disperse it or use it. If used constructively, it can bring about resolution. If left unchecked it can, over time, kill you. No wonder it has a bad rap.

> **People with tempers and anger issues are at higher risk of heart problems.**

While we are entitled to feel angry, we are not entitled to use it to damage others. When your anger is used as a weapon, your boundaries will be unguarded and need more anger to feel secure and safe. Not honouring your own anger calls out the furies, weakens your defences and only fuels the need for more anger.

Similarly, if you cannot bear to have anger in your life or you repress it, you weaken your boundaries. Pretending you are not angry just turns the fury inwards.

People who invoke anger in you are often boundary impaired themselves. A counter-attack just increases conflict and hostility.

Rather than being an expresser or a repressor of anger, it is more useful to channel it constructively. If you ignore anger or don't reflect on its meaning for you, you weaken yourself and limit the expression of some of your feelings.

Physical signs of anger

Anger doesn't come out of the blue; there are always signs before people erupt:

- jutting jaw
- clenching fists
- muscles tightening
- face flushed or feeling hot
- fixed stare/glare
- frowning/eyebrows knitted together
- tight stomach muscles
- lose sense of where you are
- can't think or even see straight
- raised or very tightly controlled voice.

What happens

Anger is usually caused by feelings of injustice, frustration or being controlled or thwarted. Anger runs on a continuum from mild annoyance and irritation to rage. Most expressions of anger stem from incidents in childhood. An echo of an early experience often provides a sensitive area that, when triggered, sets off the feeling of anger. We can hold anger within ourselves for a long time. Some people hold on to it for life.

Anger in the brain

Before you have even had a moment to notice the traffic light turning green, the car behind you honks its horn to hurry you along.

Anger begins in your amygdala, where it identifies threats and raises your alarm levels. This happens so efficiently that we are often angry before we realise it.

Ideally, the frontal cortex and the amygdala interact with the frontal lobes reminding the amygdala of the inadvisability of reckless actions. However, the amygdala can disregard consequences and potential punishments and become carried away in the moment.

Neurotransmitter chemicals, known as catecholamines, give you a burst of energy that often causes you to leap into action. Your heart rate accelerates, your blood pressure rises and your rate of breathing increases. Your face may flush with colour as increased blood flow enters your arms and legs in preparation for physical action. Your attention and visual field narrows, becoming locked onto the target of your anger. Soon you can pay attention to nothing else. In quick succession, additional brain neurotransmitters and hormones are released that trigger a lasting state of arousal. You're now ready to fight if you need to.

What you can do that helps

Learning how your anger manifests itself is part of the process of using it to work for you and not against you. Discovering what triggers you to feel anger and what that anger means will help you use it as a constructive force, and not be beholden to it.

As we know, anger helps create and reset our personal boundaries. It signals what is important to us. It causes us to ask: 'What must be protected?' This in turn can help you identify what the real issue is and where it stems from. It is also helpful to consider what needs to happen for us to no longer feel angry.

Awareness about what triggers your anger and the ways in which you feel it increases your control over it and your ability to choose how to behave. Ask yourself where in your body you first feel anger. Is it in your head, face or gut? Generally, people report different first sites for their anger, including their stomachs, fists, necks, jaws and foreheads. What is the first thing someone else would notice about you if you were getting angry? Most people can tell when someone is getting angry by recognising or identifying facial signals, such as the 'look'. It's often in the eyes.

Helping children with their anger

Children often struggle with learning to control their anger. Young people can be asked the question: 'If your anger was a cartoon character, an animal, a colour or a shape, what would it be?' Asking kids to draw or paint their anger can also be useful, as is asking them to give their anger a name. A helpful assignment can be to ask kids to draw a map of their school and home and to keep a record for one week of all the places where their anger takes over. This will help them identify what is happening in their world to create angry feelings and why.

Some other questions to consider in relation to learning about and using our anger constructively include:

- When did you begin to notice that anger had taken over your life?
- Do you think the anger has always been there? (If yes, has it been a problem from birth? If yes, which one of your ancestors do you feel is genetically to blame for you having this problem? In Bali, the local healers or Balian consider issues such as anger to be a reflection of unresolved issues from their ancestors. Their treatment of issues often involves small rituals that acknowledge and appease the needs of past elders.)
- How completely do you feel anger has taken over? What sort of person are you without the anger?
- How much of your life is being run by the anger and how much is being run by you?
- Have you ever been able to stop the anger from coming on? Are there people with whom or situations in which you never feel angry?

- How could you attract the anger? What sort of animal/person/ monster is this anger?
- Do you think the anger has taken as much of your life as it is going to take? How do you predict your life will turn out if the anger gets a hold on you? How do you predict your life will turn out if you beat the anger?
- Who would be most surprised if you were to beat the anger?

How to calm angry people

Sometimes it is not you who is angry but someone else. And if you are in the way, watch out. When I was working as a psychologist in hospitals, I often had to deal with very angry people. I developed a method that helped me and may help you. I have written about this method in my book *Tricky Conversations*, but it is worthwhile repeating it briefly here.

The RESOLVE method stands for:

- **R** Respond with respect
- **E** Engage
- **S** Seek understanding
- **O** Observe feelings
- **L** Lower the tone
- **V** Value-add
- **E** Empower

Respond with respect

The aim of RESOLVE is to respond rather than to react. If we react to an angry person, we are being led by their actions. Responding involves leading angry people towards calmness.

The key in calming angry people lies in respect. Feeling respected creates the sense of being heard and increases trust. Feelings of trust reduce anger. When we respond respectfully we enable angry people to calm down and recover.

Engage

Clever thinking will keep you safer and get you further than toughing it out. As 80 per cent of communication is non-verbal, what you do is more important than what you say. Respect an angry person's space – a cornered rat fights hardest and dirtiest. Standing at an angle of roughly 45 degrees with your right side forwards rather than directly facing the person can help keep a situation calm and non-adversarial.

Hold your hands in front of you to communicate calm authority. People's feet often give more information than their faces. Usually feet point in the direction the person is most likely to move next. A shift in the direction may give you an early warning that someone is about to run away, leave or move closer to you.

Maintain at least one and a half arm's length distance from the angry person. This is less likely to increase the person's anxiety. You will also reduce danger to yourself by giving yourself time to react to sudden moves.

Position yourself so you are safe. If you can, place something between you. Find safer ground. If they back away, slowly retreat also. If they start to come back, stop and wait.

Seek understanding

Listening and validating concerns communicates respect. Validating doesn't necessarily mean agreeing; it means acknowledging the distress or upset behind the immediate issue. If one person refuses to struggle or engage in the conflict, there can be no conflict.

If someone approaches you looking irate, be the first one to talk. Say, 'Hi, you look upset about something. Do you want to talk about it?' Acknowledging their feelings at the outset prevents the person from feeling the need to *prove* how they feel, by demonstrating it.

It is impossible to simultaneously calm someone down, get them back onside and convince them that the whole thing is not really your fault all at the same time.

If you try to verbally explain or defend yourself while trying to calm the other person, you will send mixed messages. It is never wise to send mixed messages to angry people. Try to re-direct their verbal aggression into a problem-solving approach. Obviously, this is sometimes easier said than done.

Observe feelings

By the time an angry person gets to you, they're already frustrated. They may not be interested in solutions and just want someone they can yell at to vent their anger.

Aim to give the message that you aren't a threat. Avoid direct eye contact – glance but don't stare. Speak only in a calm voice. If your own feeling of anger rises, remove yourself and restart later.

Lower the tone

Try to lower the level of tension, stimulation and adrenaline by breathing evenly. Do not make a joke. People who are angry cannot be joked out of it. People may increase their anger if they feel they are not being taken seriously.

People often stop yelling when you calmly and quietly ask, 'Could you please speak a little slower? I'd like to understand.' Repeating back to the other person what was said is another way of doing this. Listen then paraphrase.

To cool things down, do something unexpected. Ask the person to sit down or step away yourself to get something, like a pen to take notes. If all else fails, excuse yourself and act as if you're about to sneeze.

Value-add

Ask, 'What would you like me to do?' This unexpected question is the most useful tool for dealing with anger. Angry people either don't know or won't admit what they want you to do. To answer this question, they will have to stop and think. To think means they will have to calm down, which is what you want them to do.

Empower

If an angry person is making you feel afraid, this is something you need to pay attention to. If you are stuck in a loop and getting nowhere, ask someone else to take over. If you really feel unsafe with someone, leave. There are no heroics in being a victim of someone's aggression.

Apathy and boredom

Cautious, Careful, Caring, Opting-out, Despondency

Listless, Inactive, Reactive, Insular, Angst, Ennui, Removed, Arrogance

'Boredom is rage spread thin.'

– Paul Tillich, American theologian and philosopher

The feeling of apathy and boredom dulls our senses. Your inner spark has been temporarily diminished. The vivid colours of life have been muted. The tempo of life has been set to low and life feels beige and uninteresting. Things appear very blah!

Short periods of apathy signal exhaustion of the spirit and create a situation where all you want to do is hunker down and recover. This can occur after a period of hostility or criticism. You are bruised by life and need time to regain your spirits. It can also happen after times of great enjoyment or achievement. Although this sudden slump in mood and energy might take you by surprise, don't worry. You don't need to be challenged by new situations all the time.

What you may notice

Apathy and boredom can be lonely feelings as they tend to isolate us. Often we don't want others to see us in our slump so we recoil from contact with friends.

Prolonged apathy and boredom can raise our levels of cynicism and contempt about things and issues in life.

Physical signs of boredom and apathy

- glazed eyes
- slumping
- tilting head to one side
- raised eyebrows
- yawning or sighing
- tiredness
- playing with or twisting hair
- eye rolling
- doodling
- chin cradling
- sleeping excessively.

What happens

When we view the world through apathetic or bored eyes, we rob ourselves of our spirit. We feel flat and bland.

Times of feeling apathetic or bored often occur in the middle of life's transitions or rites of passage. In a previous book, *Your Best Life at Any Age*, I wrote extensively about the common transitions that happen for all of us. Interestingly, a transition will occur about every seven years throughout our lives.

Rites of passage have a sequence of stages:

1. Separation from your normal way of living.
2. Liminality, a stage of being betwixt and between, or all at sea.
   This is often a time of confusion.
3. Return and re-integration.

Many of the great works of literature follow this structure. The first stage, separation from your normal way of being, may be an actual event that alters your life, such as a trip, a reunion, missing out on a promotion or opportunity or re-meeting a past love. Most importantly, it is an internal event. You are shedding the skin of your previous identity to expand into a new way of being.

The middle phase is liminality. This is a time when people are often seriously confused. They don't know which way to go. The certainties of life have vanished from view and one way of coping is to retreat temporarily into apathy and indifference.

The final stage is return or re-integration. This is about making sense of the experience and finding a new you. The entire process of a rite of passage varies in length – for some people it can occur swiftly; for others it can take time. One common experience is that it is unsettling. It is a time when things feel jumbled and don't make sense.

The bored brain

When we feel apathy and boredom the patterns of brain waves in our frontal lobes alter. The right frontal and left frontal areas of the brain activate, but for different reasons. Left frontal activity increases when people are looking to stimulate themselves by thinking about other things. The right frontal activity is increased when people are feeling negative emotions or becoming more anxious. Generally speaking, it appears that people who are good at coping with boredom are more active on the left. Those who don't cope as well with times of boredom have higher levels of activation on the right.

What you can do that helps

When apathy and boredom are visiting our lives, wonder and beauty are absent. Some of us feel sad. This is the time, even though you might not see the point of it, to venture into nature. Walk by the sea, hike into a mountain range, watch a sunrise or sunset, or sit by a gliding river.

Mix it up; change your routines for a while. Take a different route to places you often visit. Increase moments of spontaneity and variation in your life. This is a good time to do things you don't often do. If you only occasionally go to sports games, musical performances, art galleries, museums, exhibitions or libraries, this is a good opportunity. Virtual exploration of sites online and travel destinations can be a great beginning, and as so many events have shifted online, there is more opportunity than ever to participate in events that may normally be hard to get to. There is no need to invite others to watch with you. Often it is best not to feel you have to pretend to be interesting company.

Increase your sense of challenge. Get some skin in the game. If you can muster up enough interest, challenge yourself to eat new foods, learn a new language or search for information on a topic you've been meaning to find out more about. Be patient with yourself.

Liminality is sacred space. If used well, it has enormous power and opportunity. If ignored, medicated or trivialised, a great possibility for your life and your future is missed. Finally, it is worthwhile appreciating the value of boredom. It gives rise to creativity, daydreaming, solitude and expanded thinking.

Appreciation

Gratitude, Beauty, Admiration, Esteem, Regard, Valuing, Honour

Contentment, Joy, Reverie, Awareness, Attunement

*'The deepest principle of human nature is
the craving to be appreciated.'*

– William James, American philosopher and
psychologist (1842–1910)

Appreciation is a form of love. When we gaze upon something with a sense of appreciation, we value it. We see it as greater than just its functions or features. We can gaze into a loved one's eyes and feel so lucky to know them.

We can also appreciate a fulfilling meal, a song or a fine wine, but a full appreciation often includes awareness of the skill involved in their creation. We can then expand our appreciation to consider the circumstances and contributions that had to happen in order for the skills to be present in the first place. Being appreciative links us to the miraculous and the wondrous in the world.

What you may notice

Appreciation opens up the horizons of our lives, whereas apathy and indifference narrow them. Thaddeus Golas, the author of *The Lazy Man's Guide to Enlightenment*, writes that nature, as well as people, have two basic states: expansion and constriction. When we are in constriction, we shy away and retreat from life. Constriction is often in response to pain. When expanding, we are at our healthiest and are open to new viewpoints and possibilities.

Generally speaking, we are mentally healthier when we see our life expanding and mentally less healthy when we see our life constricting.

Physical signs of appreciation

- eyebrows raised
- extended exhalation of breath
- looking at the sky
- smiling
- exuding a sense of happiness or contentment
- calm demeanour
- relaxed stance.

What happens

The modern world values commerce above all else. As such, it reduces citizens into customers by utilising algorithms to find ways to sell specific products to different groups. Add to that an intolerance for indecision, confusion and an impatience with people taking the time to explore who they are and what they really want, and you end up with a world that appreciates people not for their diversity but for their ability to fit into a neat category.

Appreciation and the brain

It's hard to resist categorisation by society, as it's one of the main ways we make sense of others around us. Being aware of the process enables us to recognise when it's happening and decide if we want that to happen to us!

The benefits of being appreciative are substantial. People who express and feel appreciation often have:

- improved immune function
- fewer aches and pains
- optimal blood pressure and heart function

- better sleep
- a higher volume of grey matter in the right inferior temporal gyrus (the folds and ridges of the brain that increase the surface area, which can result in better cognitive function).

What we can do that helps

Appreciation is not a product you can buy. There is no app, program or series of steps to follow to increase appreciation. It is a stance that you take and, in time, it can become part of your lifestyle.

Don't fit yourself into a wrong shape

In a society that increasingly wants to push square pegs into round holes, be unclassifiable. Reject the categories placed upon you by others. They are figments and limitations found in someone else's imagination.

What is appreciated, appreciates

People get more of what they look for in life. If you look for misery and despondency in the world, you will find it. If you look for limitations and obstacles, you will find them. If you look for love and wonder and delight, you will be amazed by what you might discover.

This doesn't necessarily mean putting your head in the sand and ignoring all of the injustices in the world. By steering yourself towards possibilities you become empowered to change things, rather than being condemned to endure them. As George Bernard Shaw said, 'There are those who look at things the way they are, and ask why? I dream of things that never were, and ask why not?'

Appreciate the treasures in others and in yourself

Seek the best in yourself and in other people. For the people who are your family, friends and romantic partners, feel lucky to know them.

Appreciate how lucky you are to be here

The fact that you even exist is extremely unlikely. The odds against your birth were phenomenally against you being here at all. Not only did all of your ancestors have to survive to maturity (and just for a moment consider the odds against that); they had to meet one another, decide to get together, then manage to produce the next generation, which in turn produced the next generation to eventually produce the wonders of you. Cultivate appreciation of your life: there are so many ways you might never have been born at all!

'If you treat an individual as he is, he will remain how he is. But if you treat him as if he were what he ought to be and could be, he will become what he ought to be and could be.'

– Johann Wolfgang von Goethe, poet and writer, 1749–1832

Betrayal

Treachery, Deceit, Falsehood, Unfaithful, Double-crossing, Violated, Traumatised

Shame, Lying, Cheating, Concealment, Sabotage, Deceitful, Devastated, Disbelief

'Stab the body and it heals, but injure the heart
and the wound lasts a lifetime.'

– Mineko Iwasaki

The feeling of having been betrayed is a lonely, soulless place. Acts of betrayal and the subsequent feelings – shock, disbelief and hurt – can rock the foundations of your world. Betrayal is an injury.

What you may notice

Betrayal can involve our romantic lovers, business partners, employers, family members, friends, work colleagues or anyone you trust. We all desperately hope not to be betrayed. Then we learn it is a fairly common experience.

Betrayal destroys trust and can make us feel foolish. It can also make us feel angry, not only at our betrayer but at ourselves as well. If we are not careful, betrayal can be the starting point for feeling deflated, bitter or depressed.

We can also unwittingly contribute to our own betrayal. Joseph Stalin, former leader of the Soviet Union from 1878–1953, once labelled gratitude a sickness that dogs have. He died from a stroke reportedly because his doctors and assistants were too scared to disturb him in case he was simply sleeping.

What happens

One of the more common forms of betrayal is when a partner has a romantic affair with someone outside of their relationship. This is the breaking of a loving, intimate trust. This sort of betrayal is a hurt that many people can never recover from. Perhaps even more hurtful is when your romantic partner has an affair with one of your friends.

Some people only desire romantic partners who are already in a relationship. Other people only feel attracted to people who are already friends of their partner. This form of betrayal is born out of greed and can be a double wounding: betrayal by your partner and betrayal by your friend.

While betrayal often signals the death of a relationship, it can also pave the way for the beginning of a painful but new opportunity. In the Christian tradition, Judas's betrayal of Jesus Christ brought about the crucifixion, which in turn led to the Christian world's redemption. Just as trust contains the seeds of betrayal, betrayal also contains the seeds of forgiveness. Love and betrayal are partners in crime.

A lesson from Ancient Greece

Euripides was one of the best-known and most influential dramatists in classical Greek culture. His tragic play *Medea* is a classic study of anger and rage in response to betrayal.

Jason is married to Medea and they have two children. Jason decides he wants to leave Medea and marry a wealthy princess. He explains that he will not abandon Medea entirely but keep her as his mistress. Jason's betrayal inflames Medea's passion into rage and destruction. She plots the murder of the new princess, as well as that of her own two children. In doing so, she punishes herself as much as she does her husband by murdering their children.

In Medea we see a woman who does not believe in noble suffering. Her pain has turned her into a murderess. Medea's revenge is total but it comes at the cost of everything she holds dear.

One way of thinking about Medea's response is that it is a misguided, destructive sacrifice. To sacrifice means to make sacred. To do this well requires awareness and some degree of ritual. Unconsciously suppressing our own needs leads to making a sacrifice without awareness. This is an unconscious trade we can make with others: if I forgo my own needs, you will supply what I need.

The cost is fury, as others often don't live up to the bargain (or maybe are not even aware a deal has been made). A common unconscious sacrifice is: 'I will sacrifice myself as long as you love me.'

The Netflix show *Dirty John* portrayed exactly the volatile situation that can arise when one partner sacrifices their own need in an unconscious attempt to hold on to the other. Based on a true story, the show portrays the life of Betty Broderick, who sacrificed her own career and life possibilities to ensure her husband became a doctor, then a lawyer. When her husband decided he wanted a divorce to marry a younger career woman, Betty's feeling of betrayal causes her to turn her rage into reckless and wild behaviour, which leads to estrangement from her children before culminating in her allegedly murdering her ex-husband and his new wife. She was charged and sentenced to life in prison.

While the temptation after betrayal is to focus yourself externally on righting the wrongs that have happened, the lesson of Medea, Betty Broderick and so many relationships ruined by violence show that is the wrong approach. It is far better and more beneficial to focus on the healing of your own wound.

> **It is far better and more beneficial to focus on the healing of your own wound.**

Physical signs of being betrayed

- upset
- hurt
- angry
- confused
- sick in the stomach
- loss of appetite
- drinking too much
- looping thoughts of revenge
- vulnerable
- physically ill.

What we can do that helps

A betrayal that has been perpetrated by others is often preceded by a betrayal of ourselves. This is a tough thing to think about but it is possible we are complicit in all of our betrayals. Betrayals only occur when we misplace our trust; we have mis-valued someone or something.

The easiest place to see this in action is in the workplace, where, after years of devoted work, some employees are retrenched or moved on and often feel betrayed and that their loyalty has been utterly misplaced.

There is a hard lesson here: do not take all of your trust and place it with someone else or an organisation. You need to be quite discerning with where you place your trust, whether that is in the workplace or a relationship.

If you have been betrayed

You gave your trust to someone who either wasn't worthy of it or wasn't able to live up to it. The question is: Will you let this dictate the rest of your life?

You could fill your mind with fantasies of the dreadful things that could happen to a person as a result of their betrayal. While tempting, it does keep you in a loop of negativity and tied to thoughts of them.

Ideally, you would absorb the hard-learned lessons and move on with your life. However, this is easier said than done. There is a period of grief to go through and this takes time. Time is needed to acknowledge the grief and the loss. Then time and care need to be spent nurturing yourself. Time also needs to be allocated to processing your changed reality. This will lead to building a new level of trust that you can live with.

There are three main ways to deal with being betrayed:

1. Feel sad and possibly become depressed.
2. Feel a bitter fury and then seek revenge.
3. Absorb the lessons and move on.

Of course, the process of dealing with betrayal can include all three.

While you are feeling hurt and, at times, vengeful, look after yourself. You have had an awful shock. It is easy to get ill at these times. Take care of yourself physically and socially.

Strangely enough, we often find it easier to forgive our enemies than our friends. This is most likely because we almost expect our enemies to betray us. It is the people in whom we have placed our trust we feel more aggrieved by if a betrayal occurs.

If you have betrayed someone

Take responsibility for your actions. Your actions were your actions. They weren't a result of something another person did or didn't do.

If you feel remorse, tell the person how sorry you are that you hurt them. Be honest and be sincere. (If you are insincere they will detect this.) Expect the other person to be angry and want to exact some form of restitution from you.

Understand the other person no longer feels safe in their relationship with you. Answer any questions they have. If they are to ever trust you again they have the right to interrogate you.

Generally, betrayal involves deception and falsehood. This is the time to be genuine, for your own sake as well as theirs. Don't make promises you don't intend to keep. Your integrity is on the line.

If you want the relationship to repair and continue you will need to work at it and make reparations.

You may decide to ask for forgiveness. You can't demand it or expect it. At best you can hope that the other person will find ways to forgive and trust you again.

How to forgive yourself after betraying someone is more delicate. You have hurt someone you care about. Make amends. Right the wrongs as best you can. It is likely that the betrayal did not reflect the best of yourself. While it can't be used to excuse the acts, betrayal often comes from the wounded parts of yourself. Get help to repair what needs to be healed within you so you don't repeat your behaviour. Help the person you betrayed heal as best you can. Then help them to have a good life.

The betrayed brain

If you are betrayed, your autonomic nervous system (ANS) revs up into high alert within a microsecond. Everything goes on threat status, adrenaline escalates, cortisol surges and your feelings shift rapidly and often. Your threat system signals your pre-frontal cortex to focus and concentrate, make rapid decisions and work out the meaning of events.

As Bessel van der Kolk beautifully states in his book of the same name, the body keeps the score. Betrayed partners often hold their pain in their bodies as aches, chronic fatigue, high blood pressure, mitochondrial disturbance, lowered immunity, adrenal failure, weight gain, diverticulitis and fibromyalgia.

Bitterness

Blame, Cold-hearted, Defeated, Exiled, Powerless

Resentment, Remorse, Regret, Loss, Hurt, Shame, Self-loathing, Isolation

'Bitterness and resentment only hurt one person,
and it's not the person we're resenting – it's us.'

– Alana Stewart

Bitterness is a form of self-sabotage. Feeling bitter is a powerful way of harming and immobilising yourself. You are left hurt and you are also left powerless to do anything about it.

What you may notice

To be bitter we have to absolve ourselves of power and place it in the hands of an outside force. When we feel guilty we can assume too much responsibility; when we are bitter we hand over all the responsibility to someone or something else.

Bitterness can harden our hearts if we let it. We can become fixated on it and in the process become blinded to any kindness, appreciation and love around us. Bitterness can deafen us to the sound of opportunity knocking on the door of our life.

Physical signs of bitterness

- preoccupation with the past
- tiredness
- dejected feelings
- ruminative thinking

- low self-care
- teeth grinding, jaw clenching
- lacklustre and unfulfilling conversations.

What happens

To give yourself over to bitterness is to condemn yourself to a life of defeat. It is a form of devotion to the past. You keep replaying the same wrongdoings, slights, missed opportunities or affronts. Bitterness is a campaign for justice that lacks any tactics and is empty of effective action.

Most of us have some times of bitterness but you wouldn't want to waste your future on it. If you just read that last sentence and felt misunderstood, good! It shows you are more devoted to your bitterness than you are to resolving it.

Right now you may be tempted to throw this book away. However, before you do that, let's examine this thought: if you are more devoted to your bitterness than to its resolution, can you be patient enough with yourself while you go through a process of reversing this? Can you hold the intensity of your bitterness and not do damage to yourself?

What you can do that helps

The world can be harsh and you have been hard done by – so now what?

Tell your truth

There is power in telling your truth. Write out or record your history of awful and unfair treatment. You don't need anyone else listening in or making suggestions. It is your truth. Refine it until you feel there is nothing that you have left unexpressed. Take some time to do this. Don't try to accomplish it in one burst. You are aiming for a polished statement that expresses exactly how you feel.

Sit with it for a time. In privacy read or hear it again several times. Weigh the power of the statement of truth carefully. Consider it. How important is this to you? How long do you want to keep being involved with thoughts of this event? Can you let this go? If you decide it is so important to you that you need to act, you might send it to the people involved or you could just keep it as a memorial of that dreadful time.

If you decide not to send it now, you can always keep it in reserve.

Move against and move beyond

Bitterness is an invitation into a bigger world. Your previous life has not been enough to sustain you. It has left you pinched and hurt. The stage you have been playing on has not been large enough for all the roles you want to play.

Rather than defining yourself by what you have put up with (bitterness), focus on who you could become.

Busyness and haste

Needed, Wanted, Important, Goal-oriented, Ambitious, Successful

Overwhelmed, Driven, Type A, Intolerant

'I wanted to figure out why I was so busy,
but I couldn't find the time to do it.'
– Todd Stocker

There is an old story about some explorers who marched into the interior of Africa with several porters carrying their luggage. In three days they had made great distances. On the fourth day, however, the porters wouldn't budge. It didn't matter how much the explorers cajoled them or offered to pay them. The porters simply would not move. Finally an exasperated explorer asked the porters why they would not move. The answer was, 'We are waiting for our spirits to catch up with us.'

What you may notice

People often live their lives as though the present moment is merely a stepping-stone towards a better moment – a means to an end. You can become so unsettled that you are never really anywhere that you are. You can no longer see people who are not rushing at the same rate you are. Other people appear as duties and obstacles to get around. You become frightened of stopping.

Busyness is like gas – it can fill up the empty spaces in your life.

A lot of people today wear their busyness like a badge of honour. We can use willpower to just get through the day and accomplish all tasks at hand. This might be getting the babies bathed and settled, all emails answered, the checklist ticked off or all three at once.

But in the rush of life, we can lose sight of ourselves. Busyness can submerge our feelings. Not being present in the moment results in our creative world being taken away. Our imagination declines.

Within our rushed lives is another life subjugated. Most of the time it sits in the shadows, but it can loom into view at interesting times – during anniversaries, when we are ill or on holidays. Often it appears in our dreams or in reverie and daydreams.

John O'Donohue, author of *Anam Cara*, suggests considering the seven main questions that have ruled your life. These might be questions like: 'How can I be a good person or partner?' or 'How can I earn enough money?' Once you have worked out the dominant questions, you may wish to consider the seven other questions that were submerged by the busyness and haste to answer the first seven.

Regardless of how powerful you might feel or how important the projects you have undertaken are, the world was not designed with your personal fulfilment in mind.

By loosening your grasp on outcomes, you are freed from innumerable worries. As the Zen teaching koan instructs, 'Hold on tight with an open palm.'

Less action, more being.

What happens

Life is an improvisational art form. Resilience is the capacity to flexibly respond to whatever life throws up at you. When we are too busy to feel and think thoroughly we diminish ourselves. We also compel ourselves to do the same things over and over again and wonder why we get the same results. The image of a hamster running on a treadmill might be occurring to you at this point.

What you can do that helps

If you want to see who is responsible for making you so busy, grab a mirror and look into it.

But I can't ...

The refrain of the eternally busy is, 'I can't slow down in case the kids get sick/the economy has a downturn/the house is paid for/I have a steady income.' Fill in whatever applies to you. These are all valid concerns but also lead to the myth of 'some day'. Some day I'll be free of this and can live my life. The sad truth is that some day never comes.

Saying to people, 'I'm too busy' means 'I'm too busy for you.' Eliminate this phrase from your life.

Stop having agendas for others

Busy people sometimes want other people to be busy with them. We need to stop having agendas for other people, especially our children.

Live your life by the compass, not by the clock

Stephen Covey's book *First Things First* contains the wonderful adage 'the main thing is to keep the main thing, the main thing'. Covey recommends listing the seven main roles in your life in a weekly diary, beginning with looking after yourself. Once a week you should write down the one thing you could do for each role in the coming week that would create a positive difference. This shifts you from a state of being reactive and busy to being proactive.

How to be a deadline-obsessed, adrenaline junkie

If stepping back is not for you, possibly stepping forward is. You can survive a high-stress lifestyle if you take the time to recover. Recovery involves sleeping well, exercising well and eating well.

Firstly, work for yourself. There are three types of workers: cats, dogs and rats. Cats are loyal to the place. Dogs are loyal to their owners. Rats are loyal to themselves. Be a rat. Be the CEO of [insert your own name here] Inc.

Run your own business. By the way, this doesn't mean not collaborating or being loyal to people, it simply means knowing whose interests come first. If you are an employee, this is even more important. Most bosses are very vague about the details. They say something like, 'Here's a job. I'm not too clear what needs to be done – you figure that out. I want it done as soon as possible and you have no extra resources to do it.'

Bosses may be a great people but they are usually not in the business of helping you develop a balanced life. If someone is able to prioritise and take charge of schedules in a better way, that would be the person you see first in the mirror every morning.

The rule of the threes

Every day take 30 minutes to plan and prioritise the tasks you need to get done. This could be the time you specify what you want to accomplish in your seven roles. If you could only do one thing in each role, what would it be?

Then look at the remaining items on your list and ask yourself: 'If I could only do one thing what would it be?'

Once a week give yourself three hours. You may choose to spend those three hours with others, but basically they are three hours you can spend entirely on your terms.

Once a month, take three days. A weekend simply isn't long enough to recover if you are living a high-impact lifestyle.

Once a year (or more if you can) take at least a three-week break. Three weeks gives you time to recover, rest and rejuvenate properly.

Don't muck around

Do one thing at a time and finish it. Learn when you focus best and preserve that time for high-priority tasks.

Allocate red time and green time to your daily schedule. Green time is time when you can be interrupted; red time is time for you to focus.

Avoid unnecessary interruptions

Turn off notifications on your devices. As soon as you pick up a device you are likely to waste time. The dopamine surge we get from finding new and interesting information on our devices resembles the rewards of hunting and gathering of our distant ancestors.

Have an individualised phone ring tone that sounds more like a gentle suggestion than a national emergency. Make the tone distinctly yours so you don't confuse it with someone else's phone. You have enough interruptions of your own without dealing with everyone else's.

Avoid unnecessary meetings

Reduce them and reduce their duration. Decline some. Leave some when your bit is done. Use email and voice messages to replace as many time-eating meetings as possible.

Physical signs of busyness

- feeling rushed
- always thinking of the next thing to do
- always vaguely unsatisfied
- poor digestion
- poor or interrupted sleep
- feeling wired but tired
- poor attention to detail
- lack of focus.

Confidence

Assured, Sure, Optimistic, Hopeful, Positive, Capable, Ambitious, Reckless

Uncertain, Hesitant, Self-critical, Self-efficacy

'Everyone should have an imaginary friend – themselves.'

– Andrew Fuller

Confidence is a form of appreciation. You value the attributes you have rather than denigrating yourself for who you are not. Confidence is one of the most powerful – and elusive – qualities that creates success in life. When we feel confident we look upwards and outwards at life. We stand taller.

Building confidence means that we develop the courage to be ourselves and to try out new things.

What you may notice

Unless we are exceptionally talented, most of us approach new activities with a slight apprehension, which might be followed by bewilderment and confusion. Our first attempts may be feeble, but if we persist, we often gain a sense of mastery.

If, however, someone rescues us when we are feeling bewildered, we learn that someone else can do what we cannot. This is why rescuing children when they are struggling with a new activity is toxic to building their confidence.

Physical signs of confidence

- direct eye contact, open face
- talking more rapidly
- being prepared to interject, make proposals and critique ideas
- holding interlaced fingers behind the head while sitting
- direct eye contact, chin up
- hands held behind back
- shoulders widening
- strong handshake
- good posture
- legs splayed, possibly taking up territorial space such as leaning against the side of a doorway
- leaning back
- smiling less.

Lack of confidence is often associated with displays of dominance. These are signals used by people who lack confidence that aim to show others how more powerful/interesting/vibrant/intelligent they are. Interrupting other people's conversation can be a sign of this as can typically arriving late (the implicit message being my time is more important than yours). Dominating a physical space with parts of the body, such as spread legs or arms, or smirking can also signal this.

Some men use handshakes that rattle your bones in order to display their dominance.

What happens

We all have an endlessly running debate that occurs between our inner critic and our inner cheer squad. Depending on who is talking the loudest, confidence ebbs and flows. For all of us there will be times when our confidence lags.

Waiting for confidence is something you can spend your life doing. It generally comes after, not before, you do something.

What you can do that helps

There is a sign in my psychology practice that reads:

> BE YOURSELF.
> EVERYONE ELSE IS TAKEN

There are several steps to creating and building confidence.

Model yourself on the best

Rather than thinking about all the things your parents did that were wrong, think about their best qualities. Remember the times when they were at their very best. Now know that you have inherited those qualities. Live with them.

Trust

Nothing builds confidence more than trust. One of the best ways of communicating your trust is to ask people for help. Requesting assistance communicates that you regard others as capable and competent. It builds a bond.

Confident people surround themselves with smart people and ask them to help out. People who lack confidence often feel the involvement of others is a threat and don't ask for assistance.

Live a bold and adventurous life

One of the best ways to develop confidence is to live an expansive life in which you do different things, eat new foods, go to strange places, see new shows or movies and try out things you wouldn't usually have a go at.

Develop a yes bias

This means developing a personal motto that generally says, 'Why not?' For example, if someone says, 'Let's go to France,' you try to answer, 'Sure, let's find out a way we could do that.' If a child says, 'I want frogs and ice-cream for dinner,' you say, 'Okay, you find the frogs; I'll get the ice-cream.'

Accept invitations if you can. You never know who you might meet or what opportunities you might miss out on if you don't go.

Don't fall into the avoidance trap

When you avoid something you fear, your fear grows. What is avoided looms larger and appears more daunting; what is attempted lessens in size. While it might seem like a kindness to help people opt out of things they are fearful of doing, mostly it just makes them even more fearful. Apply this to yourself when you are faced with something you are afraid of doing. You don't eliminate your fear before doing the fearful thing; by doing it the fear should lessen automatically.

> 'It is not because things are difficult that we do not dare.
> It is because we do not dare that things are difficult.'
>
> – Seneca, ancient Roman Stoic philosopher

Follow the 80:20 rule

No one is confident about everything all the time. We all have hesitations and setbacks. Aim to be bold and confident about 80 per cent of the time. In many areas of life, it is the predominant pattern that counts in the long term.

Know that first past the post isn't always the best

The person who can achieve a skill first is often not the best at that skill in the long term. In fact, there are considerable advantages in being a little bit older when you start new activities, as you bring a whole lot of previously learned skills and experiences with you.

Set probability goals

A probability goal is a challenge that includes an error margin. For example, you might say to yourself, 'Let's see if I can throw a ball into a hoop seven times out of 15 throws.' As you become more skilful you might then increase the challenge of the task by moving the hoop further away and say, 'Okay, it's harder now. Let's see if I can throw the ball into the hoop nine times out of 20.'

Probability goals help us learn how to challenge ourselves and also make it less likely that we will give up if we don't get 100 per cent first time.

Little steps lead to giant leaps

Most highly skilled and confident people deliberately practise skills that they are not good at. They go out of their way to put themselves in challenging situations so they can become more skilled. For example, top golfers often put golf balls into the trickiest part of a bunker so they have to develop the skills to make those shots. People only learn to deliberately practise things that they are not so good at when someone has told them that they believe in them and that mistakes are the only way to get better at something. If we can't learn to make mistakes, we can't learn to improve. People who don't make mistakes do not usually make anything.

When we focus on our learning strengths we build the confidence to tackle areas where we are not so capable. One way to do this is to assess your learning strengths at my website: www.mylearningstrengths.com.

Build a have-a-go culture

People often express their insecurities by claiming that they can't do something or by comparing themselves negatively with others. For example, 'I am the world's worst dancer' or 'I'm no good at maths.' When someone makes comments like these, acknowledge their feelings. Ask them what makes them feel that way. Accept their fears or insecurities as genuine but don't agree with their self-assessment. For example, you might say, 'I get it that you are struggling at maths; now how can we work on it to make it easier?' Confident people make plans to improve in areas they initially find difficult.

Be on a continual treasure hunt

Devote your life towards looking for the best in yourself and in others. Focus on successes, skills and abilities. Be resolutely positive and follow the role model of Thomas Edison who, after trying 10,000 times to develop an electric light bulb, said, 'I have not failed. I've just found 10,000 ways that won't work.'

Do more, think less

Winston Churchill commented that a pessimist sees the difficulty in every opportunity, and an optimist sees the opportunity in every difficulty. Confidence is the gathering together of the best threads of yourself and having another go.

Brains and confidence

When we are feeling confident we have higher levels of serotonin (our natural antidepressant) and gamma amino butyric acid (GABA), which both help us feel calm and assured. Our interactions with others are usually more reciprocal, resulting in increased oxytocin (the hormone of trust and connection) and lower levels of stress hormones.

Contempt

Discerning, Righteous, Moral, Certainty, Superiority, Disdain, Scorn, Smug, Arrogant

Dislike, Wariness, Spiteful, Racist, Sexist, Hateful, Condescension, Sneering

'Nothing so needs reforming as other people's habits.'

– Mark Twain

Contempt is the intellectual version of disgust. To be contemptuous is to belittle things. It can reduce marvellous things to the bland and commonplace. It robs the magic out of life. Left unchecked it can belittle you.

There is an affirming sense of righteousness in the feeling of contempt. It allows us to sit high and mighty above the unwashed and seemingly inferior masses and hold forth with our opinions and judgments. The follies and the shortcomings of humanity are laid bare to our all-seeing clinical eye.

What you may notice

When people display their feelings of contempt they generally contort one side of their face into a smirk or sneer. This is often accompanied by rolling of the eyes, a twisting of the lips and an all-knowing shrug of a shoulder. Usually they look away from the object of their contempt towards a not-quite-equal but at least aware compatriot.

Contempt takes us into the world of one-upmanship. What fun to be at the top of the tree, morally speaking!

There is just one minor glitch to all of this smug superiority: what we often find contemptible in other people is a projection of what we can't abide in ourselves. It is such a shame to realise this. It ruins all the fun when you know that behind your contempt lurks a deep, insecure form of self-loathing. Even worse, you may realise that when you climb onto your high horse, you show everyone else your bum.

What happens

Contempt can be a denial of humanity and a source of justification for bullies, racists and sexists. In the attempt to elevate yourself in superiority, you lessen someone else. Contempt is a diminishing emotion. By making other people smaller than they truly are, you also make yourself smaller.

Contempt reduces life to a measuring stick. The life of a contemptuous person is diminished to a ledger sheet of comparison and assessment. There's not much space for beauty in there. The best things in life are not quantifiable. Also, pumping up your own tyres at someone else's expense only means you are bound for deflation.

Some politicians are good at using contempt to manipulate and create division in society. Lacking the vision and perhaps the will to create a better future for citizens, they instead find some group to serve as a scapegoat for why people aren't flourishing as they believe they should. Of course, it is women and minorities of all types who sadly bear the brunt of this.

What you can do that helps

Unless you hold the position of judge in a legal court, don't take on the role. No-one has in their possession the internationally validated measurement tool of life. Stop assessing and measuring and start enjoying. Open your eyes to the best in others and allow their less desirable attributes to float under your radar.

Remember, there are no negative feelings. There are only feelings. So of course there are times when contempt can be useful. There are some actions and attitudes that warrant derision and contempt. If you can use your feeling of contempt not to sit back and judge but impel yourself towards better ways, then you will be making the best use of it.

The contemptuous brain

Contempt is the opposite of kindness. Feeling contemptuous means you do not appreciate that other people have different feelings, values and situations to your own. The ability to perceive different people's perspectives is known as theory of mind. The parts of the brain that enable us to look outside our own situation and see the situation of others include the medial pre-frontal cortex, the precuneus (involved with memory, integration of information, perception of the environment, and pain response), the superior temporal sulcus (language perception to simulating the mental processes of others) and the temproparietal junctions (social conditioning). Contempt also links to feelings of disgust and is often associated with activation of the insula (which receives sensory experience from the environment).

Courage

Heroic, Adventurous, Bold, Reckless, Fearless, Risky, Negligent

Thoughtless, Terrified, Goal-driven

'Promise me you'll remember you are braver than you know,
stronger than you seem and smarter than you think.'

– AA Milne, *Winnie-the-Pooh*

Courage is a matter of the heart. Moral courage is being authentic even in the face of disapproval or rejection. It is about doing the right thing regardless of what others might think. It takes courage to stand out from the crowd.

What you may notice

Eighteenth-century German philosopher Immanuel Kant coined the phrase 'ought implies can'. This implies that if we are able to act for the greater good, we should. Courage is a lot like doing the right thing for the greater good, even when you don't want to or feel afraid. It is living by the golden rule: treat others as you would like to be treated.

Courage is often associated with physical heroic acts. However, it can also be an interior act. It takes great courage to look inwards at your own feelings and desires and examine the darker corners of yourself.

What happens

We develop moral courage by being around people who showed us how to live this way. Firstly we were able to trust and rely on them. Then we were helped to see that others also trusted and relied upon them. Then we were helped to see that other people rely on and trust us. It is hard to be morally courageous if you have never seen it in others.

To see someone stand up for an idea or a principal and defend it publicly against others who are less courageous can be life changing.

When people are interviewed after doing courageous acts and are asked why they acted the way they did, their response is often that it was instinctive. If pressed for more details they will often answer, 'I didn't really think at all; it just seemed like the right thing to do at the time.'

Somewhere in their upbringing they absorbed messages about caring for others and being courageous so that it became not what they do but who they are.

Ideally, we would give every young person the experience of standing up for a belief in the face of opposition, and also participating in creating positive change. These are lessons that aren't about thinking as much as feeling and doing.

Common features of morally courageous people

- They see themselves as linked to others through their common humanity.
- Where the rest of us see a stranger, the courageous see a fellow human being.
- Where some of us see categories of people, they see individual people.
- They believe their actions will make a difference.
- They know how to act.
- They ask themselves how they could make a positive difference to a situation.
- They stand up for people who can't stand up for themselves.

Most people want to have courage but are too scared to try and develop it. They hope for it in their political leaders, they want it in their friends and family, and they also aim for it in themselves. The opposite of courage is conformity.

Courage is related to integrity. There is a solidity to integrity. It stands for something.

People seek out integrity. They want meaningful ideas, people and actions on which they can rely. They want to relate to people they can believe in. Integrity is the quality that answers the question, 'Can I rely on you to do the right thing?'

People also want to act with integrity and often feel ashamed when their actions don't match their words or ideals. The times when we lose integrity are often the times that haunt us later on. Pausing to think before taking an action helps us to maintain our integrity.

Reputations are often ruined when people lose integrity by not acting honestly in accordance with their expressed beliefs. It can take courage to maintain our integrity.

What you can do that helps

Courage has nothing to do with not feeling fear. It is about recognising the contribution you can make to creating a difference in the world. It requires a recognition of your own personal power to make a difference. It is not reckless or foolish but it is determined.

Some things to think about

- Think about the contribution you can make.
- Don't wait for others to make your contribution for you.
- Take on a stance of leading the changes you want to see rather than following others.

You are the leader you have been waiting for

Ideally, one day you will realise that you are the leader you have been waiting for. Gandhi's much cited quote that you must be the change you wish to see in the world is apt here. My friend and colleague Stephen Brown often uses the question: 'What would you do if you were 10 per cent braver?'

From bystander to upstander

Someone who stands up for what they believe in is often called an upstander, as opposed to being a bystander, where you just watch things happen. Being an upstander is an act of social bravery. It takes courage to withstand the power of mob thinking and act according to your values.

It is easier and more comfortable not to be an upstander. Why think for yourself when you can get everyone else to do it for you? To act with integrity is not the most popular position in the world but remaining sane in a crazy world requires it of us.

Integrity is doing what you say you will do and being who you say you are. It is something we look for in governments, friends, family members and, most of all, in ourselves.

When we act with integrity we get to know the best of ourselves. When we seek out the best person we could become, we help ourselves to be that person.

Think in terms of relationships

Feelings and actions cluster together, especially when there is more than one person involved as there is a contagion effect between people. That means there will always be a temptation to allow things to slide past your moral compass because it is easier to fit in and not make a scene.

People largely do what they see others doing. This means that people will copy you and what you do.

We all run the risk of behaving shabbily occasionally. When someone calls us to a higher standard we almost inevitably rise to a better standard. Know that you are strong and that it is easy to underestimate yourself and your power.

Expand your impact zone

When we come across a problem or an event, we might think to ourselves, 'Oh well, someone else will deal with it.' Climate change is a good example here. By doing this, not only are we are undervaluing the impact of our actions, we are actually collapsing time. When we move on rapidly and never think of the incident again, we are reducing the time we have to influence the issue, and that time period is a lot longer than you might first think. Elise Boulding, well-known for her writing and research on peace, suggests expanding your time, rather than condensing it.

This is how you can expand your impact zone:

1. Think of the oldest person who touched or cared for you when you were a baby.
2. Try to work out what year they were born (guess if you need to).
3. Now think of the youngest person you have touched or cared for.
4. Imagine them as great, great grandparents. What year will that be?

The difference between the earliest year and the year in the future is the time period of your direct impact. Most of us live approximately in a 200-year time zone.

Increasing your impact zone both backwards and forwards will help you to think more clearly about the consequences of your actions. You are able to honour those that have come before and contribute to those who will come later.

Remember the three rules of politics

1. Everyone makes mistakes.
2. Covering up the mistake is worse than making the mistake.
3. Everyone forgets rule number two.

The courageous brain

A protein called stathmin, which works in the amygdala, an area deep inside the brain that produces fear and anxiety, seems to have an important role in courage. When courageous people step into action, their adrenaline often increases, reducing their sensitivity to pain and fear, and energising their actions.

Curiosity

Interested, Friendly, Inquisitive, Captivated, Intrigued, Puzzled, Avid, Alert

Nosy, Meddling, Interfering, Fascination

'The mind that opens to a new idea never returns to its original size.'

– Albert Einstein

Curiosity is a broadening, expansive feeling. Where boredom and disinterest shut us down, curiosity awakens us. When we are curious, we look upwards and outwards. Our interest is piqued. We are alert and on a voyage of discovery. We connect positively with the outer world.

What you may notice

The sensation of curiosity is linked to wonder and awe but is a distinct feeling. Just as an itch often creates an urge to scratch our skin, curiosity causes us to be intrigued and think differently.

What happens

Being curious places you on the side of coming alive. One of the common features of depression is a lack of curiosity. The return of curiosity, along with an appreciation of beauty, is a common sign that depression is lifting.

To be truly curious about your inner self takes courage, but the rewards are great. In the process of looking inwards you might discover the shamed, humiliated and possibly even traumatised parts of yourself. These concealed parts can often subdue you in daily life without you realising it. By acquainting yourself with your unknown parts, you are discovering the hidden treasures that will ignite and animate your life. Sometimes, in therapy sessions, I witness people fight tooth and nail not to be curious. They are intent on not discovering or acknowledging the hidden parts of themselves. I find that curious!

What you can do that helps

Just like Alice in Wonderland, become curiouser and curiouser. Develop the art of being intrigued. This is very simple. In a world that is preoccupied with facts and answers, become more interested in questions. Rather than working to find answers, search for and ask questions that no-one else has ever thought about asking.

Become a people detective

As you move around in your daily life, pick random people and try to work out what they are feeling, what they might be doing and what they could be thinking about. Not only will you increase your skills as a spy, you will also increase your emotional intelligence.

Watch magic and illusionist shows. Trying to figure out how a magician goes about altering the perception of an audience can be fascinating.

Become interested in differences of opinion

People hold such different positions about all manner of things: religion, culture, justice, politics. Try agreeing with one position one day and then the opposing view the following day before deciding on your own viewpoint. Read articles or books that support your viewpoint and then try to find a counter-argument or evidence to the contrary.

Value questions more than answers

Dream up interesting questions to consider. Some examples include:

- Why did dinosaurs die out?
- Will cockroaches be the last living creature on this planet?
- If you could time travel, where would you go first? Why?
- If you could invent a new form of travel, what would it be?
- If you could redesign the human body, what would you change?

Déjà vu

Homecoming, Return, Mystical, Spiritual, Insightful

Perplexed, Unsettled, Unnerved, Reminiscent

'Right now I'm having amnesia and déjà vu at the same time …
I think I have forgotten this before.'

– Steven Wright

Déjà vu is an unsettling feeling that has a dream-like quality. In our daily lives we rely on the certainty of what is familiar to us and what is unfamiliar. When those two states become confused, we feel perplexed.

Déjà vu means 'already seen' in French. It occurs out of the blue, when you get the strange feeling of having been to this very place or done this very thing before and you know you haven't. You have a sense of familiarity about something that shouldn't feel familiar. This happens to most people at some point in their lives.

What you may notice

Déjà vu is an experience more than a feeling. It is almost like your unconscious is trying to remind you of patterns it has recognised before. It is a spooky feeling.

Near Levadia, in Greece, flow two springs called Lethe (the river of forgetting) and Mnemosyne (the river of remembering). In Greek mythology the souls of the newly dead drank from the river of forgetting so they would lose all memory of their past existence in order to achieve reincarnation. The more initiated souls were taught to seek the river of remembering so they could achieve enlightenment. Intriguingly, these two rivers ultimately flow into each other. Perhaps déjà vu is a mix of our own forgetting and remembering.

What happens

No one knows for sure what causes the feeling of déjà vu. It could be that your memory system becomes so interconnected it provides you with false information. At best, your memory is a reconstruction of events. We all try to reconstruct experiences using fragments of reality interlaced with things we make up. We all have unreliable memories. Also, we are all so suggestible, especially between eight and 12 years of age. The idea that bits of information become jumbled between the did happen/might have happened/never happened categories is not that surprising.

It is thought that there may be two aspects to déjà vu. The first is a misrecognition of what is familiar as what is not. The second is a misremembering of what has been experienced as what has been imagined or thought about.

If you have ever sat down with your brothers or sisters and recalled times past, there are often as many versions of the events as there are people in the room. The strongly held opinions about who has the correct perception of events demonstrates how we all create our memories differently. Since everyone can't be correct, someone must be misremembering.

People experience déjà vu more frequently if they have epileptic seizures, suggesting some involvement of the temporal lobes (located above your ears). Some people with epilepsy experience déjà vu at the onset of an epileptic seizure.

The temporal lobes are sometimes referred to as the 'God spot'. Electrode stimulation of these areas of the brain indicate they are associated with mystical experiences, spirituality, interpretation of social situations, temper outburst and suspicion.

When experiencing déjà vu, some people not only feel like they have been in a particular place or said a particular phrase before; they also feel able to predict what is going to happen next or where specific items are placed.

Physical signs of déjà vu

- confused
- bewildered
- light-headed
- surreal
- spaced out
- shivering
- skin tingles
- things move in slow motion.

What you can do that helps

Déjà vu is a common and harmless experience. It can be useful to ask yourself: 'What does this remind me of in my past?'

Our memory is a creative act and déjà vu helps us to be aware of this. Our reconstruction of our life's history has some vague spots, some definite times and probably some events that didn't actually occur at all.

Most of the time we have a firm grip on what we think reality is. We pick out the main events of our life and create a story or narrative around those happenings. This is selective and there are some parts of our lives that are completely overlooked or dispensed with as they don't fit the dominant story.

There are also times when we merge what happened with what we wish had happened. We creatively weave stories about our lives and then we believe them. At times we are like a child who swears black and blue that they have brushed their teeth when all of the available evidence points to a contrary interpretation.

You can use this knowledge to concern yourself that you probably haven't been totally in touch with reality for years. Alternatively, you could see the freedom in this by allowing yourself to re-write parts of your personal life history in ways that are more constructive and kinder to yourself.

Just one word of warning: while our déjà vu may give us a sense of being a high Egyptian priestess in an ancient dynasty, I wouldn't rush to claim ancestry until you clearly see your name written on a pyramid.

The brain and déjà vu

Déjà vu has to do with the way you process and recall memories. This involves our hippocampus, which is embedded deep in our temporal lobes (above our ears), and the lower part of the brain, the cerebellum.

One circuit monitors our ongoing experience of the outer world. The other retrieves past memories. If the two just happen to occur at the same time, the simultaneous activation compresses time between the two brain functions, causing us to remember the present or experience déjà vu. No one is exactly sure what causes this to happen but stress, lack of sleep and travelling can all be triggers.

Desire and attraction

Want, Interested, Flirtatious, Playful, Caring, Loving, Love-struck, Lustful

Infatuated, Obsessed, Discombobulated, Stalking, Craving

'There are two tragedies in life.
One is to lose your heart's desire.
The other is to gain it.'

– George Bernard Shaw

Desires are shifty things. They can be quirky and flighty. Love, addictions and obsessions are much more dependable. They stick around. The flighty nature of desire could explain why after a day of longing for healthy fresh salads, we end up at 11 pm with a chocolate bar and an ice-cream in our hands.

Our primitive wanting brain always wants more but also wants it differently. What you desire in the morning may evaporate by lunchtime, only to reappear in the late evening. Often this is ascribed to the weakening of willpower throughout the day. More likely it is just our desire shifting.

To be at the mercy of your desires can be like a dog trying to go for a walk but being distracted by enticing smells along the way. Let your mind off the leash and it wanders around trying to sniff everything at once.

What you may notice

Observing your wanting mind gives you a clue into the distractions that could divert you from the things you feel are really important. Your primitive brain wants you to be safe and it wants you to be comfortable.

It doesn't like doing too many of the hard things. In fact it delegates them to the more developed thinking brain.

For example, you know you need to prepare for an important meeting the next day but the latest episode of your favourite Netflix show has just dropped. You really want to watch it. In fact, your wanting brain is yelling that you need to watch it! If you give in to that desire then there is a good chance you will turn up to your meeting without having done the work. Yet your work is important to you. So why is your brain trying to distract you? Because the reward for watching is much stronger than doing work.

We can also have unrecognised desires. These are things we want even though we don't know that we want them. Advertising is based on exactly this part of human nature. It offers little tastes of desirable states and repeats them over and over again. The most effective advertising links unrecognised desires with more frequent human wants. For example, many people want to be popular, and if they are told that buying a particular product will have crowds of admirers hovering around them, it is more likely that they will buy the product.

Your desires can trap you. Buddhism teaches that desire is a sure pathway to misery. Giving in to all your desires is to be dominated by your latest whim and can have you running like a hamster on a treadmill. This is the reverse of impulse control where your frontal lobes help you do the hard stuff first.

There are a lot of things people desire to have in life. This is mostly a positive thing as these desires push us towards useful things such as jobs, working hard, saving for something special, or buying a home.

Desire is also a first step towards romantic love. There is a wonderful discombobulation that comes with a new attraction to someone: your world changes. You lose your grip on productive undertakings. Your mind becomes like a magnet drawn to the person you desire. Desire is responsible for that heady, unforgettable experience.

Industries have been built and fortunes have been made on making people more desirable. The effort placed into becoming more desirable threatens to rule the world. In the animal world, the display of secondary sexual characteristics, such as a luxurious tail, large strong antlers, vivid plumage or demonstrations of strength, are all used to show off how virile, attractive and worthy of attention some (usually male) animals are. Then you look at the proliferation of nail treatment centres, beauty salons, gyms, flash cars and expensive watches and wonder if there is any real difference at all between us and the animal world!

Physical signs of desire

- casting longer, more frequent looks
- locking eyes with someone
- one shoulder rises while the head tilts towards it
- pupils dilating
- blushing
- heart racing
- slightly increased perspiration
- mirroring of the other person's posture, such as crossing legs in the same way and direction.

What happens

What we desire mostly is a change of state. From thirsty to quenched. From hungry to fed. From sad to happy. From childless to parenting. From single to being in a relationship.

Most desires have a life span. They begin with a trigger that causes a minor shift in neurochemical balance (often an increase in stress hormones or a depletion in the neurochemicals that help us with happiness (ie serotonin) and motivation (ie dopamine).

In his book *The Power of Habits*, Charles Duhigg helped to outline the sequence of habits that create feelings of desire. A trigger sets off a change in neurochemical balance that kick-starts a sequence of behaviours that result in a reward.

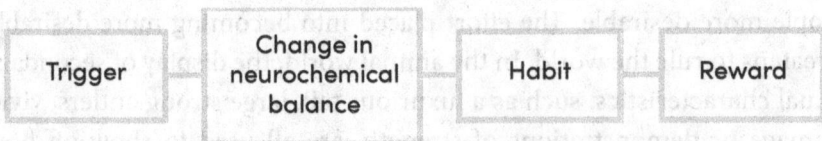

Trigger	Change in neurochemical balance	Habit	Reward

Let's go through a typical scenario. You are lying on the couch after a long week. You feel exhausted but you have kept to your goal of working out and eating less. An advertisement comes on for your favourite chocolate bar. Your levels of dopamine and serotonin deplete. You think, 'I can't have it.' Your levels of cortisol increase: 'But I want it.' Your dopamine kicks in with anticipatory delight: 'You've been sooooo good this week.' Your resistance has been crushed by force of habit and off you go to the cupboard.

What is real and what is imagined are experienced similarly in the brain. This means that delaying the reward for a while sometimes works, especially if you give yourself a substitute reward (ie every time you want a chocolate bar you go read a chapter of a good book or go for a walk or just do something else instead).

Alternatively, you can imagine giving yourself a reward. You can be like someone on a barren desert island imagining themselves sipping a fine French champagne.

Pausing before giving in to a desire and doing something else for 20 minutes can be helpful. For example, you might say to yourself: 'I can still eat the chocolate cake but first I'll do twenty push-ups.' You might find that your motivation to keep to your goal has strengthened during the exercise and you no longer want the chocolate bar. Or it has become easier to resist, at least. See? Desires are so fickle!

What you can do that helps

Desires are contagious. We tend to desire what other people desire. This is the basis of fads. If someone influential admires a celebrity or a brand name, other people are in turn more likely to desire it too.

One of the great paradoxes of yearning, attraction and desire is that we are drawn to people who desire similar outcomes to ourselves. We want others to love what we love and desire what we desire but as soon as they do, they become competitors. Rene Girard, the French philosopher, called this memetic desire.

People who desire the same thing have a sense of similarity and connection. As long as they can share whatever they desire they remain the best of friends. As soon as they cannot, they can become fierce rivals and the worst of enemies.

Of all the things we desire, probably the two most worth trying to have are more time and better health.

The desiring brain

Our brains seem set up to enjoy the pursuit of pleasure more than the attainment. We focus more on the pot at the end of the rainbow than the rainbow itself. Our wanting brain is one of ceaseless desire. As soon as it receives a hit of dopamine from anticipating a reward, it is off on some hare-brained scheme to find the next pleasure-filled, dopamine-soaked moment. This makes contentment a very transient feeling. Just as you have fulfilled one desire another pops up to take its place.

This is why focusing your life on happiness is bound to leave you feeling flat and dejected. As our brain desires new pursuits it may be best to give it many to follow-up on. Broadening the number and range of meaningful quests you embark upon will keep your brain entertained, while not allowing you to become too deflated when your desires are fulfilled.

Disappointment

Realistic, Dispirited, Morose, Sombre, Unmotivated

Dejected, Let-down, Disillusioned, Surprised

'I started out with nothin' and I've still got most of it left.'

– Seasick Steve, from the song 'I started out with nothin"

Disappointment is part of an adventurous life. Situations won't always work out, people won't always be sincere or reliable and you will let yourself down.

What you may notice

Disappointment stems from the best part of us, the part that hopes for the best and wishes for better. It is a heavy feeling. Things have not worked out as we wanted. Plans are dashed. Dreams are squashed. When we wish to bring out the best in ourselves and other people and don't achieve it, we feel disappointed.

Close relatives of disappointment are frustration and avoidance. Frustration is a little like a four-year-old's tantrum: 'I've got to have it.' Avoidance is the mental game of saying, 'Well if I can't have it, it's not worth having anyway.'

Physical signs of disappointment

- pupils constrict
- eyes filled with tension
- exhalation with lips left slightly open
- looking away and downwards
- muscles sagging.

What happens

> 'The mark of the immature man is that he wants to
> die nobly for a cause. The mark of the mature man is that
> he wants to live humbly for one.'

– Wilhelm Stekel, Austrian doctor and psychologist, 1868–1940

Disappointment about the past and its hurts can blind us to life's opportunities for happiness. Become less interested in your disappointments.

Enthusiasm and disappointment often contrast with one another. Enthusiasm originates from two Greek words 'en' and 'theos'; the word enthusiasm literally means 'the god within'. When we feel disappointed we become dispirited. We lose our inner spark or sense of being animated. We are dampened down and diminished.

When we are disappointed, we need to reacquaint ourselves with our own inner creative spark. Feeling bummed and let down is a product of our hopeful expectations. Of course we could choose to tone down our dreams and become blasé about what life has to offer. Perhaps it is more productive to become more focused on the process of life and experiences unfolding, rather than the outcome.

What you can do that helps

You don't need special skills to get through a disappointment. You just need to know what you should do.

Some things to think about

Before you feel too disheartened by people's responses, remember the loudest boos always come from the cheapest seats. Consider whether others would dare do what you have tried to do.

How not to turn a disappointment into a disaster

What most people do when faced with a disappointment is … nothing. They become so overwhelmed by the event that they freeze up, retreat or do mundane things.

A disappointment is often equated with a life-threatening event when your coping skills are overwhelmed. If you interpret it as a disaster, your body switches to combat mode. Keeping perspective and not converting a disappointment into a disaster empowers you to have options and possibilities.

Knowing the difference between a disappointment and a disaster can literally save your life. In disasters, events happen faster than you can process them. If you turn every disappointing setback into a disaster you spend your often shortened life on red alert. If you act like everything is at stake, pretty soon, everything will be.

Check in on yourself

Ask yourself:

- 'Is this a disappointment or a disaster?'
- 'Does someone have the equivalent of a gun at my head?'
- 'What options are available to me in this situation right now?'

Go for a walk

Move. Clear your head. Physical activity produces natural endorphins that can make you feel happier.

How to process information

Get above the problem. Map or draw the problem. Try to create a bird's-eye view of the situation. Think, 'This is awful but it is not the entire world' and 'The way I feel now is not going to be the way I will always feel.' As dreadful as the situation may be, it is essential that you be realistic about it.

Develop a strategy

Having worked in crisis services and situations, I estimate that in most disasters, about 75 per cent of people freeze up and become immobilised. About 15 per cent can think and act clearly, while the remaining 10 per cent are so gung-ho they are simply dangerous.

Trusting your instincts alone to survive a disappointment may cause you to either fight back or flee. Neither are good strategies. Careful consideration, option-seeking, and soliciting astute outside advice offer more probability of successfully coping with a disappointment than the randomness of from-the-hip decisions.

Things to consider:

- During a disappointment, it's important for people to feel that leadership is connected and in touch with the situation.
- If everything is a priority then nothing is a priority – narrow your focus to increase your impact.
- Balance short- and long-term goals – in difficult times everything demands attention, but people try harder if they have a sense of a better future.

Weave the tapestry

Hollywood movies love to promote grit and rugged individualism but there are times when you will need to have a team of up to six people directly involved in assisting you to steer the situation.

Outline the situation as accurately as you can and ask for input as well as any additional information people might have.

As a team, consider the best options. Seek group agreement. Leadership is making happen what you believe in.

Nit-pick problems early

While it sounds negative, it is worth considering the worst possible outcome of a potential situation. This prevents you from being taken by surprise and disappointed in the result.

You may not base your plans on a pre-mortem, but it will help you to be prepared. Rehearse in your mind all the things that could go wrong. This allows you to anticipate and get organised. However, do not fall into the trap of thinking that because we can imagine these outcomes they are likely.

Using this process, we surpass our competitors who are shocked and fall back, devastated by what they did not imagine coming. It also allows us to plan for win-win outcomes where we can.

Allocate roles

Delegate areas of responsibility (eg prevention, communication, caring for people who are upset). Agree on a time to reconvene and discuss.

Keep relationships in mind

The relationship between the adults in any family, organisation or team situation is powerfully impactful. That relationship is reflected and amplified throughout. Bear this in mind when you are discussing potential disappointments or the outcomes of one. We all have setbacks on the path to success. Help each other rebound by supporting each other and assist others to make the contribution they can make.

Anticipate that people will pitch in

Difficult times can bring out the best and worst in people. Some people will think they have nothing to offer unless you personally ask them to help. Other people will want the event over and done with as soon as possible. Continue to make requests of these people. Others still will want to process dreadful events over and over. Support these people until they can resume their usual way of functioning.

Always bear in mind that it is your desire for better things that is the source of disappointment, so don't allow it to rob you of hope.

Disappointment and the brain

Disappointment is a feeling that coincides with sudden decreases in serotonin, dopamine and endorphins.

Two neurotransmitters – glutamate and aminobutyric acid (GABA) – are released simultaneously by neurons in a small region of the brain called the lateral habenula to signal the emotion of disappointment. It appears that the more glutamate is released relative to GABA, the greater the disappointment signal the brain receives.

Disgust

Righteous, Scared, Fascination, Derision, Sickened

Appalled, Dislike, Aversion, Distaste, Repugnance, Revulsion, Abhorrence, Loathing

'The greatest pleasures are only narrowly separated from disgust.'
– Marcus Tullis Cicero

There is a wisdom in repugnance. Disgust is a universal emotion that protects us. Ranging from dislike to abhorrence and loathing, it causes us to withdraw and avoid. It is such an essential part of us that it occurs deep in our midbrain and in our bodies. Disgust can save our lives and, as such, has great value.

What you may notice

Disgust originally helped us to avoid physically threatening situations where food supplies were dangerous. This is why it is a contagious feeling. If one of your ancestors ate some bad food and vomited, everyone else felt nauseous and therefore did not eat that food.

People who are feeling disgusted by something will usually try to reject, expel or remove the offensive object or substance so that they will not come into further contact with it.

Physical signs of disgust

Due to its high survival value, we have many ways of signalling disgust:

- curling of the upper lip
- lump in the throat

- retraction of the chin with an almost dry-retching motion
- nausea
- aversion to eating or drinking
- avoiding eye contact
- nose wrinkles upwards (to close nostrils)
- vomiting
- turn head away
- shut mouth and eyes.

However, what repels us can attract us! What disgusts us can also have an alluring quality. This is why some of our most desired perfumes often mimic the scent of bodily by-products.

The enduring fascination people have with monsters, serial murderers and gory details plays into this disgust/attract pattern. This might be, in part, related to our fear of death and our desire to conquer it. While this applies to us at any age, it explains why children's literature is filled with monsters in wardrobes, trolls under beds and bridges, wolves who dress as grandmothers and evil witches who lure innocent children to untimely ghastly ends.

Dealing with what disgusts us on a metaphorical level also delights us. This is why some people will go a long way and put a lot of energy into being appalled and disgusted.

We speak about disgust in interesting ways, such as 'That makes me feel sick', 'There is something rotten about this' or 'I wash my hands of the whole affair'. It is very physical language.

What happens

Over time, our feeling of disgust has broadened from a biological mechanism to help us avoid poisoned food to our perceptions of other people. When we respond with disgust to others, we begin to dehumanise them. We start to think of them as objects less than ourselves. It's easy to lose perspective when inflated by a sense of superiority and/or self righteousness. Interestingly, it is the things we are disgusted by in others that we are secretly disgusted by in ourselves.

The disgusted brain

The insular cortex is the main brain structure involved in the feeling of disgust. It is involved in the processing of all the foul stimuli you have ever experienced. If you tell a story of someone being mistreated or stabbed in the back, the insular cortex activates. If you describe something rotten that you have done, the insular cortex activates. If you see someone vomiting, the insular cortex activates. The same part of the brain activates regardless of whether it is physical or moral disgust being felt. The same part of the brain activates for physical disgust as it does for moral disgust.

When we interact with others socially, our brain's medial pre-frontal cortex (mPFC) is active. Social neuroscientists Susan Fiske and Lasana Harris found that the mPFC was less active when Princeton undergraduates were asked to make judgments about marginalised groups such as the homeless or people with substance-use disorders. Furthermore, this lowered mPFC activity was coupled with brain responses indicative of a disgust response. So it seems a combination of insular cortex activation and lowered mPFC is involved with the feeling of disgust.

Disgust is powerfully involved in us-and-them thinking, which is the basis of sexism, racism and violence. People tend to divide other people into groups who are like themselves, ie us, and those other creatures who bear no similarity whatsoever, ie them.

People do this based on their perceptions of two personal characteristics: warmth and competence as explained in the table opposite.

There are people we see as being high in warmth and competence and, as we like to also think of ourselves that way, we classify them as members of our group, or us.

There are people we think of as being high in competence but low in warmth. They are seen as conniving, cunning people whom we fear and also envy.

There are people we categorise as being high in warmth but low in competence. We tend to view these people as easily taken advantage of, dupes. Our main feeling towards them is one of pity.

Finally there are people we view as being low in both warmth and competence. As they are nothing like us (we think!) we reject them and feel disgusted by them. We try and avoid them at all costs.

This has major implications for the world, as well as for you personally. As soon as we think of people not as individuals but as representatives of a group (eg all men, all women, all cyclists, all motorbike riders etc) the type of thinking described in the table kicks in. This is the basis of sexism, racism, prejudice and violence.

	Warmth High	Low
Competence High	**Us** Feeling: Acceptance	**'Cunning' them** Feeling: Fear/envy
Low	**'Sweet-hearted dupes' them** Feeling: Pity	**'Pathetic' them** Feeling: Disgust

What you can do that helps

It is interesting that disgust readily spins into self-righteousness. Awareness of our own propensity to judge, and our subsequent withdrawal and avoidance behaviours towards the other person, gives us pause for thought and a chance to reconsider our actions.

Sometimes social disgust stems from our beliefs and values. Sometimes this is because we feel it is warranted and worthwhile (eg disgust at abusive behaviours to people or animals) and sometimes it is because it can be damaging and harmful (eg racism, homophobia, shaming of people because of appearance or disability).

When disgust towards a group of people falls into areas outside clear social standards, we can try to think of them as individual people rather than as members of a group. By rehumanising, rather than dehumanising, we can temper our disgust and have more power over our behaviours.

Embarrassment

*'The rate at which a person can mature is directly proportional
to the embarrassment he can tolerate.'*

– Douglas Engelbart

Sir Arthur Conan Doyle, the author of the Sherlock Holmes series of books, once sent a telegram as a joke to 12 friends that read, 'Flee! All has been discovered.' All the men were well respected in society. Apparently, Doyle was shocked to learn that within the next few days, all 12 men had left the country.

The Greek philosopher Sophocles remarked, 'There is no witness so terrible, no accuser so powerful, as the conscience which dwells within us.'

What you may notice

Embarrassment is not a casual emotion, one you can shrug off and think, 'So what, I'm embarrassed now.' If you try to do this, you are likely to blush more vividly.

The feeling of embarrassment is linked to shame, social anxiety and guilt, but it is also a distinct emotion with unique physical signs played out on the body.

We might feel ashamed of our dancing skills and anxious about what others will say about our style of dancing, but also guilty because our partner loves to dance and we are reluctant to join in. To top it off, we can feel embarrassed that we have all of these feelings!

Complicating matters even further, we can feel just as embarrassed by being complimented or admired as by slipping and falling in public.

Embarrassment changes what people do. It is a powerful teacher. Most of us would travel a long way and complete a whole range of unpleasant tasks rather than repeating an act that is likely to give rise to this feeling. Embarrassment doesn't bring about forgiveness; it creates avoidance.

Anyone who has mis-stepped and stumbled knows that ruse of trying to make it look purposeful in the hope that no one else notices. Waking up after a night of alcohol-fuelled singing at a karaoke bar where you wowed the crowd with a rendition on Sinatra's 'I did it my way' will do it. Most people also know the dreadful realisation that comes when something they have done is cause for acute embarrassment. Embarrassment exists on a continuum from blushing to mortification and humiliation.

In some societies, embarrassment was equated with a loss of face and a dishonouring of one's family. Sometimes it has been seen as worthy of exile or death.

Many of these features are seen in the modern cancel-culture where people are socially ostracised (the most painful form of bullying) for social misdemeanours.

Upsetting someone without intending to do so, or asking for a possession to be returned or a salary to be raised, can send some people into a squirming mass of embarrassed insecurity. Many people also dread difficult conversations not just because they lack conflict resolution skills, but because they find them to be acutely embarrassing.

What happens

From having a guest enter your messy home to spilling drinks, having feelings of sexual desire, forgetting someone's name and most bodily functions, we seem to find no end of things to be embarrassed about.

Hearing their own singing or speaking voice is enough to send some people into a spiral of self-consciousness. This is why the thought of public speaking (let alone public singing) mortifies so many people.

You don't even need someone else to notice what you have done to feel embarrassed. Anyone who has ever dreamed they have shown up at work or school naked knows that embarrassment can occur even in our sleep!

The usual expression of embarrassment includes looking down, smiling or attempting to control or inhibit the smile. Embarrassed smiles differ from happy smiles. In a happy smile, the corners of the mouth are pulled up and there is crinkling around the eyes. In the embarrassed smile, the lips turn up but the eyes don't crinkle.

Typically, an embarrassed person will avoid eye contact, lower their chin, smile and then shift their gaze to the left. This is suggestive of right-hemisphere brain activation associated with withdrawal behaviours. People frequently touch their faces when embarrassed, or look away to the left.

Of course, the other key indicator of embarrassment is blushing. Some people blush when they are embarrassed and others feel embarrassed by blushing. Facial reddening can occur during other feelings as well. Blushing begins with a sharp increase in blood flow followed by a slower rise in facial temperature. The increase in blood flow is what causes the actual appearance of the blush. Other physical changes can include a rise in blood pressure and fluctuations in breathing.

Others are likely to detect our blushing well before we are aware of it ourselves. Beta-adrenergic receptors of the sympathetic nervous system appear to play some role in facial blushing.

Embarrassment and the brain

Although no one particular area of the brain has been identified as the site of embarrassment, there is a thumb-sized bit of tissue located deep in the right hemisphere of the front part of the brain called the pregenual anterior cingulate cortex, which is thought to be integral to the feeling of embarrassment. This region of the brain is responsible for regulating many automatic bodily functions such as sweating, heartbeat and breathing but is also linked to many thinking-related actions, such as reward-searching behaviours and decision-making. If the pregenual anterior cingulate cortex becomes damaged (as in people with dementia), it can make people far less prone to feeling embarrassed.

What you can do that helps

It can be helpful to be aware of the three main functions of embarrassment.

Firstly, embarrassment is a powerful social signal of appeasement. It is a sort of get-out-of-jail card. It is showing, 'Don't be too hard on me because you know I am giving myself a hard time about this.' It also signals, 'I am so sorry and I really, really, really didn't mean it.' It is clearly saying this mistake was not intended.

People who blush after committing a faux pas are viewed as more trustworthy than those who do not. Children who appear to be embarrassed by an action are less likely to be admonished by parents.

People often find it useful to confess that they are nervous and easily embarrassed before speaking to an audience. It often elicits kindness from the listeners.

Rather than hiding away feelings of embarrassment, learning to express them can help. Part of the reason we find the cartoon character Homer Simpson so lovable is his famous expression of frustration with himself: 'D'oh!'

Secondly, embarrassment lingers long. We don't forget these moments easily. We dread re-experiencing this feeling and avoid whatever behaviours triggered the state. Some excruciating episodes of embarrassment have caused people to serve longer sentences than many serious crimes. It is a form of social pain. Being aware that carrying past humiliations may be restricting your life is useful. Some past misdemeanours should have a use-by date. Becoming kinder and more forgiving of yourself is needed.

Embarrassment lingers long.
We don't forget these moments easily.

Thirdly, embarrassment activates us to restore our esteem in the eyes of others. Find ways to get beyond the original event. Make amends if need be. Apologise to those that you may have hurt even if you never intended to do so. If that is not practical, devote yourself to a personal cause that helps victims to heal and recover.

Be aware that some people's sensitivity to embarrassment can be so strong that they place their wellbeing at risk. Being able to say no, getting some medical check-ups, buying products that keep you safe and well are all essential. If you are squeamish and avoidant about doing any of these things, ask someone else to act as your guardian angel by reminding you how to overcome your embarrassment and to look after yourself.

Envy

Admiring, Deferential, Imitating, Inspired, Longing, Coveting

Overlooked, Furious, Hating, Discontented, Dissatisfied, Desiring, Trapped

'Of the seven deadly sins, only envy is no fun at all.'
– Joseph Epstein

Envy is unhappiness about the success of someone else or what they have, while secretly feeling inferior at the same time. Most of us are so concerned about concealing our feelings of envy that we never speak of it. Envy is a secret and surreptitious emotion, which is why we often experience it as a twinge of envy, rather than permitting ourselves to display it openly.

What you may notice

Envy differs from jealousy, which is when we fear someone will take away something we possess. Envy is when someone has something that we want. Jealousy is based on fear of losing something; envy is based on coveting something.

To live in a world of envy is to be trapped in endless negative comparisons. It is a world where you want things not because they are important to you but because someone else has them. To resolve envy is to become free to live the life you want.

Although we may try our hardest to hide it, our envy slips out in funny ways: in sarcastic comments, 'joking' insults or 'funny' bullying. Look out for people who praise you without their eyes lighting up.

Physical signs of envy

- a rigid body
- clammed or clenched teeth
- mouth/lips tightening or constricting
- urge to wash hands or shower
- fainting
- squinting
- put-downs
- sarcastic comments
- belittling.

What happens

In today's competitive world, envy is actively promoted through the wonders of marketing. We live in an age where there is a common belief that if someone gets something good, someone else misses out. More emphasis is placed on who gets the biggest slice of the pie than on developing a bigger pie for everyone. This is especially promoted in countries where there is a greater inequality of distribution and income. The idea of prosperity for all is discarded in favour of a world of haves and have-nots.

Envy can cause you to work harder and harder for longer and longer to buy things you don't even want. Envy is not associated with the concept of enough. That is why it is toxic to contentment.

Social media amplifies envy. Through all the advances in digital platforms – Facebook, Instagram, SnapChat and WhatsApp, to name just a few – we can look into other people's lives in way that no previous generation could. FOMO (fear of missing out) is a form of envy.

If you are envious of someone, you may want to put them down, as though this will raise you up or lower everyone else's opinion of them. But it just doesn't work. There is a golden rule:

> You can't make yourself look good by
> making someone else look bad.

Just to make things more complicated, you can also inherit envy. Your envy does not always belong to you. Your envy of others can originate from what your parents envied or admired.

You are not supposed to show that you are envious. Revealing feelings of envy is generally frowned upon. We want to push ourselves and other people towards nicer, more acceptable emotions. This may cause us to miss the message that our feelings of envy are trying to tell us ... and the most important one of all is that it is time to look after yourself.

We can also envy ourselves. When we think we are not as successful as we have been or are not being rewarded as well as we have been in the past, our dopamine levels drop and we become less motivated.

What you can do that helps

When the grass appears greener on the other side of the fence, it is time to water your side of the fence. Rather than enviously desiring what others have, consciously develop an awareness of your own wants and tastes.

You can only swim in one swimming pool at once. If my friend owns a swimming pool, do I need to buy a swimming pool? If my friend has a beach shack, do I need to have a beach shack? The point here is if our friends do better than us, we are often the beneficiaries of that success.

It is fine to want some of the things or characteristics that others have. It can motivate us. At its best it can bring out the best in us. But there are dangers.

Envy has many manifestations and some of them are hidden dragons. For example, it is possible to envy another person but confuse it as feeling attracted to them. Thus, you can fall in love with what another person has – status, money, power, family ties or intelligence – rather than with who that person really is. This can also be true for competencies. We risk confusing our envy of someone who handles a number of things well with desiring them as a person. This is almost always a disastrous relationship. By the time you come to your senses you may experience some animosity toward them for the envious feeling you hid from yourself.

If we don't see our desires clearly, we can assume someone else has all the good things while we are left with the scraps. People idealise what they are envious of. The comparisons that form the base of envy are usually a mirage; we overvalue what someone else has and undervalue what we have.

We can also become so focused on envy that we don't develop our own talents. We may even give up on our own talents. To be free of envy is to be truly free to become yourself.

> **We can also become so focused on envy that we don't develop our own talents.**

Eleanor Roosevelt once said, 'No one can make you feel inferior without your consent.' When you envy someone else, you are giving them a compliment. But it's a compliment that can harm you and how you feel about yourself. In order to neutralise your envy, you will have to diminish the source, elevate yourself, or do both.

The world seems to love measuring the relative worth of things and comparing. To lessen or neutralise envy, you need to give up comparing yourself with others. This is true independence of spirit.

Take the time to develop your emotional intelligence. Know that there are many different types of people, many ways to be successful, and many ways to be smart.

Work out what you really value and want in life. Many people don't spend enough time thinking about this and instead sentence themselves to lives driven by comparing their progress with others.

The brain and envy

Envy activates the areas of the brain associated with pain perception. When you see your friend's holiday pictures posted on social media or learn that a colleague was promoted above you, a part of the brain called the ventral striatum is activated. The ventral striatum is part of the limbic system and is involved in decision-making and reward-related behaviours.

The anterior cingulate gyrus is also likely involved in envy, because it processes empathy, emotion and decision-making. This could be why envy feels so painful.

Equanimity

Balanced, Composed, Aware, Imperturbable, Detached

Perceptive, Centred, Wise, Considered, Cool-headed

'Equanimity arises when we accept the way things are.'

– Jack Kornfield

Equanimity is a state of stability and composure in the midst of changing circumstances or feelings. The word originally comes from the Latin adjective *aqueous*, meaning level or equal. 'Equanimity' is a combination of *aequus* and *animus* in the Latin phrase *aequo animo*, meaning 'with even mind'.

What you may notice

Equanimity is the capacity to not be caught up with what happens to us. It is the ability to see without being caught by what we see. It is calm presence rather than indifference, aloofness, rigidity or complacency.

Being able to rise above the moment is a wonderful gift and can be a difficult state to attain. Often in life, we either get swept up by pleasant and enticing events or become agitated by unpleasant, undesirable occurrences. We then enter a fantasy world where we wish for a day when all problems will disappear and the good times will go on and on.

As the Buddhist tradition tells us, the problem is not the ups and downs of life but our attachment to them.

The eight winds that buffer life

From the writings of the Japanese priest Nichiren Daishonin, we can learn that equanimity is the ability not to be buffered by the eight winds of the world. These can distract us from what we think is important.

106

The first four, which we generally tend to like and seek out, are:

1. **Success:** gain and prospering
2. **Fame:** receiving honours or accolades
3. **Praise:** being praised or admired
4. **Pleasure:** enjoying gratification

The remaining four, which people tend to avoid, are:

5. **Failure:** suffering loss
6. **Disgrace:** being humiliated
7. **Criticism:** being criticised or disparaged
8. **Pain:** experiencing physical or mental suffering

Becoming attached to or excessively elated with success, fame, praise or pleasure can be a set-up for suffering when times change. To experience success is wonderful, but if it leads to arrogance, we have more to lose if or when we struggle later on. To seek fame is often to attempt to live up to a false identity and hide our true self from others.

Similarly, if we become too associated with failure, disgrace, criticism or pain, we often give up, feel despondent and avoid. Equanimity protects us from the vicissitudes of praise and blame, success and failure, pleasure and pain, fame and disrepute.

Pulling rabbits out of hats

If we depend too much on praise, our primary purpose in life can become all about pleasing others. We might also become anxious or conceited by beginning to believe our own publicity. Alternatively, we can become so inflated by the praise of others that we fear losing their regard. Our lives can become controlled by what other people think of us, rather than what we actually want.

The favourable winds offer only temporary forms of happiness. After a short-lived experience of contentment we are out trying to achieve the next 'win', the next level of fame and recognition, the next compliment or the next indulgence.

Being chased by the demons of failure

The less favourable winds do not offer refuge either. If we identify ourselves as having failed, we may label ourselves as incompetent or inadequate. Often we will avoid areas and experiences where we feel we could fail again.

In our attempt to avoid disgrace we can become compliant, secretive and sometimes shamed. In an attempt to do nothing wrong, we might end up doing nothing at all.

No one likes criticism, but if we base our lives on avoiding it, we can't grow into the people we could have otherwise been. Positive feedback and constructive criticism actually help shape us into the strong, resilient people we need to be. Imagine if a young child or toddler was never told not to do something or shown a better way of doing things. What sort of adult do you think they would grow up to be?

When we are faced with pain, our reactions can become avoidant, disconnected and discouraged.

Avoiding being buffeted by the four less desirable winds might appear attractive but it is rarely possible. To attempt to avoid these often requires a narrowing of life and its opportunities.

If we can realise that our sense of inner wellbeing is actually independent of the eight winds, we are more likely to develop equanimity and live with a balance of heart.

What happens

Let's explore the experience of equanimity through the lens of resilience.

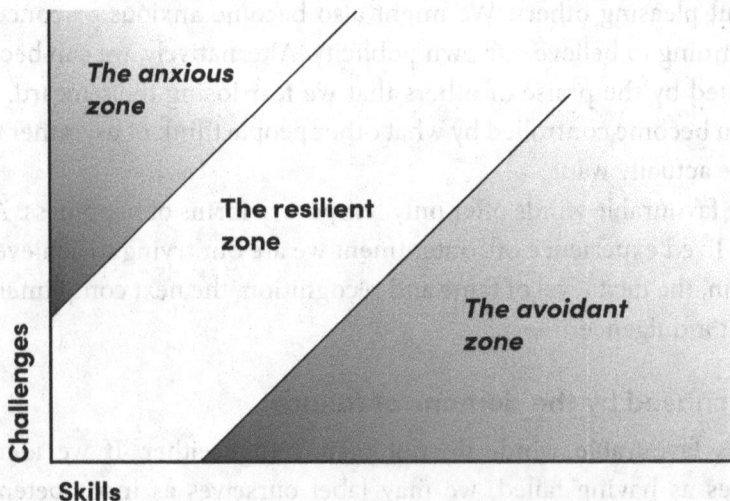

The anxious zone

The resilient zone

The avoidant zone

Challenges

Skills

There are three main states of resilience:

1. the resilient zone
2. the anxious zone
3. the avoidant zone.

Sometimes we explain this concept to children by using the Goldilocks parallel of being too hot, too cold or just right.

The resilient zone

This is where a successful life and positive relationships occur. There is a balance between the challenges or problems we have to face and the skills we have available to meet them. It is in this zone that we can attain equanimity. We can also learn from others while being aware of ourselves in this zone.

The anxious zone

When the challenges or problems we face exceed our skills, we may become anxious, agitated, thoughtless or aggressive. We are ruled by fear and stress and become rattled and overwhelmed. In this state, we are usually unfocused and unable to learn from others. While we feel acutely aware of our anxious feelings, we are limited in our general awareness.

The avoidant zone

When our skills exceed the challenges we face, we can become bored, disinterested and listless. If we add stress to this mix, we give up, can't be bothered or think, 'What's the point?'

We can easily see stress as being in an agitated state, but avoidance and absenteeism are also expressions of stress. When we are avoidant we don't want to stand out. We seek escape routes to avoid life. In this state we are often defensive and unable to learn from others. Ways to escape and avoid issues include illnesses, overuse of social media, work, inability to commit, job failures and distancing yourself from intimacy.

When we are out of the resilient zone we know it. We don't feel right. People are almost always trying to do the best that they can to get back into the zone. We are all healthier and happier in the resilient zone than out of it.

What you can do that helps

Start by noticing any of the behaviours or characteristics that signal you have fallen out of the resilient zone. In our close relationships, we can learn what signs show us that our partners are either anxious or avoidant and work out ways to enable them to get back into the zone.

While most of us instinctively know when we have fallen out of the resilient zone, the ways we try to find our way back in often don't work. Even worse, some of the strategies *seem* to work but not for very long. Ineffective methods include arguing, yelling, drinking alcohol, working too hard, flirtation with others and checking social media for long periods of time.

You may know this from your own life. There are days when you feel edgy and need to step away from the issues of life to regain your composure. Or your partner comes home feeling overwhelmed, grumpy and snappy. These are the times when you need to think about what your partner needs to get back into the resilience zone. You might say: 'Take it easy/have a seat on the couch/have a cup of tea/do you want to talk about it?/don't worry I'll fix dinner.' By doing so, you give them space to get back into the zone.

Alternatively there might be times when you or your partner have been kicking around the house a bit bored, a bit listless and a bit restless. Here you might suggest: 'Let's go out/catch a movie/go for a walk/visit friends/or have a picnic.' By doing so, you have brought them back into the zone.

Try to remember a time you noticed that you or your partner were upset. What helpful things did you do to get back into the resilient zone?

When we are in the resilient zone we can learn, be present and mindful and make good decisions about our lives and relationships. The more time we spend in the zone, the more positive and creative we are. Not only that, but more time in the zone means our immune systems function better so we also tend to live longer.

**The more time we spend in the zone,
the more positive and creative we are.**

When we are anxious and agitated we are too wired and frazzled and reactive. When we absent ourselves from life, we are not involved. We are overly passive, sullen, sad, dejected, defeated, tired, or just too defensive to be with people.

The more time all of us spend in the resilient zone, the happier we are. The more time our relationships spend in the zone, the more satisfying they are.

There are skills that we can learn to help ourselves return to the resilience zone. There are skills that we can learn to use to help others to be in the zone most of the time.

Equanimity is a state of graceful balance. It is a state of being in the world but not being defined by it. The world offers us all a torrid rush of rewards and punishments, highs and lows that can have us going up and down emotionally like a yo-yo.

Your restless mind wants the best for you. However, being restless, as soon as it achieves something it is busy chasing the next accomplishment.

In the midst of rush and turmoil, maintaining wise attention and being able to see and think beyond the limits of current circumstances allows all of us to remain flexible and resilient.

While some experienced meditators may be able to sustain the state of equanimity, most of us find the forces of life to be irresistibly compelling. Learning to detect the signs that we are in an anxious or avoidant zone and discovering how to return to the resilient zone is a major advantage in life.

Failure

'Theory is when you know everything but nothing works.
Practice is when everything works but no one knows why.
In our lab, theory and practice are combined:
nothing works and no one knows why.'
– Albert Einstein

Failure is putting a full stop where you should place a comma instead. At the place where people should write Act Two, they more often than not write The End.

The feeling of failure often brings with it a sense of deficiency, inadequacy and disappointment in yourself. It can also be associated with shame and you may want to give up, quit, and avoid the situation. We attach considerable amounts of our self-value to our performances and when we see ourselves as not succeeding, we become harsh judges of ourselves, feel shame and are often frightened of repeating the experience. This ranges from spelling the current number of words in the early years of education to having the best retirement plan in the later years.

Failure can hurt you. There can be fury in failure, as we frequently beat ourselves up emotionally over it. Or it can kickstart success. Resilience is the ability to flexibly respond to whatever life throws at you. Adaptability and readjustments are necessary as we all go through life.

Often it is the people who have been lucky enough to have early experiences of success or have never experienced a setback or failure who are the most vulnerable to being gobsmacked when a failure (inevitably) occurs.

Children who grow up with hardships are often tempered and street-hardened by their experiences. One woman told me, 'I grew up in Stalingrad. After that there was nothing else life had left to throw at me that could make me feel bad.'

Some of the most self-reliant people grew up in orphanages. As the saying goes, if you want to be a rock star, have an unhappy childhood. No one wishes hardship on children but we can't ignore the fact that failure has lessons to teach us.

In her book *Unchained Memories* psychiatrist and author Lenore Terr interviewed a number of prominent people who had experienced failure and trauma as children. While they reported they wouldn't have chosen what happened to them, they all acknowledged that they gained valuable insights and lessons they may never have received otherwise.

Statistically, failure is much more likely to happen than success. There are usually more ways to get something wrong than there are to get it right. Some people with an area of skill and aptitude become incredibly self-denigrating about their inability to succeed as well in other areas of life.

> **Statistically, failure is much more likely to happen than success.**

Other people collect areas in their life where they can fail: not finding a partner, not getting good marks at school, not earning enough money, not getting a job, not getting a promotion, not getting another promotion. Quite often they think they only have one way to succeed.

What you may notice

It is a common idea that we learn more from our failures than our successes. Failure is an essential part of learning.

Learning something new can be like trying to complete a jigsaw puzzle when you've lost the box and have no idea what picture you are trying to create. All the time you are attempting to put the puzzle together you are thinking, 'Other people can do this more easily that I can!'

All learning is science

When we help students who have anxiety about failing, we tell them that all learning is science. In science what we do is gather together all the relevant information to form a best idea called a hypothesis. We then conduct experiments to test if that idea is indeed the best idea. Those experiments might involve chemicals, surveys, reading or research. Depending on the results, we either then confirm our hypothesis or develop a new one. In science there are really no failures; there are just experiments that either reveal better ideas or do not. If you can take the position of being a scientist conducting experiments, it helps you to see failures as part of the process of learning. The best part about this is that you can be a scientist at any age.

What you can do that helps

One issue with failure is that it is often so scary that we don't take the time to look it fair and square in the eye. It helps to think about failure and success as a continuum.

Failure   Success

Where would you place yourself currently on the line above?

A common error that people make is to think that in order to be successful they need to be good at everything. The problem is that none of us are good at everything. We all have learning strengths and we all have areas that are a relative struggle. The trick is to use what we are good at to leverage our success in other areas. This requires us to stop blaming and start planning. You can do this by going to my website (www.mylearningstrengths.com) and analysing your learning strengths.

At the time of writing, over 25,000 people have used this to create pathways towards success.

Looking failure in the eye exercise

Most people find the previous activity difficult to do because there are areas of success and relative failure in different aspects of life. Most likely you are a combination of both. Here is another way you can look failure in the eye:

Ask yourself:

- What would absolute total success look like for you? Describe it.
- What would abject failure look like for you? Describe it.
- Now work out a percentage of the probability of each:
  - What per cent is the likelihood of total absolute success? 20%, 50%, 80%?
  - What per cent is the likelihood of total abject failure? 20%, 50%, 80%?

For a moment, imagine yourself as a total abject failure. Now develop your own personal rescue plan. Start to consider how you begin again to create the building blocks of success. How would you tip the balance back in your own favour?

After doing this exercise, you still won't like failure. You'll still fear it – we'll explain why when we discuss fear in the next section. However, at least you will know in your thoughtful mind that even if failure occurs, you will find a way to rise above it.

Most great things have very simple beginnings. An idea or concept is refined and built upon over time to become what it ends up being. Pop star Adele took over six months to write her chart-topping song 'Hello'. Bob Dylan spent two years on his famous 'Tangled up in Blue'. JK Rowling was rejected by over 20 publishing houses before her Harry Potter series was accepted. She once commented that hitting rock bottom was the basis for her success.

No one plays 'Bohemian Rhapsody' perfectly on their first try. They fumble around making mistakes that they refine as they go. Leonard Cohen took five years to write his now world-famous song 'Hallelujah'. He apparently wrote over 80 draft verses, and in one writing session, he was struggling so much that he sat on the floor in his underwear and banged his head on the floor.

It is far healthier to think, 'Well if most wonderful things had very simple beginnings, I am a fairly simple person therefore I am capable of creating great things.'

'The man who achieves, makes many mistakes, but he never makes the biggest mistake of all – doing nothing.'

– Benjamin Franklin

You have to get things wrong in order to get them right. Creativity and discovery are about getting something wrong, then shaping it and honing it until it becomes something wonderful.

Fall down seven times and get up eight

Adopt a motto of always getting up one more time than you fall over. Almost everyone used this approach to learn to walk. You fell over, got up, fell over again, got up again. If you are able to walk today the reason is you got up one more time than you fell over.

The failed brain

When we experience a win, our brains release endorphins, dopamine and serotonin, which combine to encourage us to repeat the experience. Tennis players often demonstrate this by urging themselves to 'Come on!' When we experience a failure, our brains release cortisol, which often leaves us wanting to avoid similar tasks.

Fear

Agitated, Apprehensive, Trepidation, Dread, Nervousness, Anxiety, Panic, Frightened

Scared, Terrorised, Traumatised, Horror, Desperation, Shock, Terror, Uneasiness

'Fear is like fire. If you can control it, it can cook for you,
it can heat your home. If you can't control it, it will burn
everything around you and destroy you.
Fear is your friend and your worst enemy.'

– Sui Ishida

Fear is not cowardice. Fear is wisdom in the face of danger. Fear will save our lives if we listen to it and act on it.

Fear doesn't muck around. It says, 'Do what I tell you to do!' The gut feeling of fear is an instantaneous process – don't ignore it. In fact, you probably won't be able to! No animal senses fear and thinks, 'Oh, it is nothing.' Properly focused fear is our intuition keeping us safe. Intuition means to guard, to protect.

What you may notice

Tuning into our fear is like having a motion-sensitive security light outside a home on the right setting. You don't want it going on every time an insect flits past. But you don't want it not to light up if a herd of bulls stampede the front door.

If our fear setting is not right, it can't keep us safe. If we fear everything, we won't react appropriately when something really fearful occurs. Similarly, if we fear nothing, we become so reckless we place ourselves at risk.

All our feelings stem from two basic positions: love and pain. Pain includes fear and stress.

Physical signs of fear

- staring
- baring teeth or grimacing to show teeth
- eyes scanning and darting before intensely focusing
- faster heartbeat
- muscles tensing or cramping
- teeth clenched
- feeling nauseous
- getting cold and clammy
- butterflies in the tummy
- raised arms near but not touching the face
- temples throbbing
- face scrunches up
- nostrils flare
- coughing before speaking (also signals reluctance)
- chin quivers
- goosebumps
- hair stands up on the skin (piloerection).

What happens

Fear is a response to something. It always has your best interests at heart. Trust your feelings of fear more than your logic. What causes alarm probably should.

Trust your feelings of fear more than your logic.
What causes alarm probably should.

Fear only sounds in the presence of danger. It is a signal to increase your awareness of what is happening around you or to you. When you honour the intuitive signals of fear you will come to trust your own sense of it. There will be no need to be wary all the time.

To simplify things a bit, you have two brains. The first is the brilliant, insightful, creative and thoughtful brain that evolved most recently in humans.

The lower part of your brain evolved a long, long time ago and forms the bottom part of your brain. This primitive part of your brain detects threats and perceives fear. It also keeps you alive, it keeps your heart beating while you sleep and it keeps you at the right temperature, so it does a lot of really important things. In fact, this lower part of your brain contains 80 per cent of your brain cells. It knows what frightens and threatens you and it is pretty much the same brain that dinosaurs had.

Your primitive brain relies on neuroception: the hunches, the tingling 'spider senses' that unsettle or unnerve us. We can't quite explain the reason we are feeling this way but we can notice it and it is powerful.

Our primitive brain can save our life. If something were to attack us, we would be running away before our thoughtful brain had even considered what to do. So while your brilliant, thoughtful brain is busy considering all the possible ramifications of what is happening, not to mention other possible interpretations and the overall philosophical implications of the event, your primitive brain already has you running out the door to safety.

The fearful brain

What's going on in your brain when you are experiencing fear? In short, a lot. Our response to fear begins in the amygdala. This prepares our body to deal with danger. The brain becomes hyperalert, pupils dilate, the bronchi dilate and our breathing accelerates. Our heart rate and blood pressure also rise.

Peripheral blood vessels (in the skin, for instance) constrict, central blood vessels around our vital organs dilate to flood them with oxygen and nutrients, and muscles are pumped with blood, ready to react.

Levels of blood sugar or glucose spike, providing a ready store of energy. Levels of calcium and white blood cells in the bloodstream also increase.

The amygdala triggers activity in the hypothalamus, activating the pituitary gland, which is where the nervous system meets the endocrine (hormone) system.

The pituitary gland secretes adrenocorticotropic (ACTH) hormone into the blood.

The sympathetic nervous system – a division of the nervous system responsible for the fight-or-flight response – signals our adrenal glands to release adrenaline into our bloodstream.

The body also releases cortisol in response to ACTH, which brings about a rise in blood pressure, blood sugar and white blood cells. Circulating cortisol turns fatty acids into energy, ready for the muscles to use should the need arise.

Catecholamine hormones prepare muscles for possible violent action. These hormones also reduce activity in the stomach and intestines, which explains the feeling of butterflies in the stomach when we are nervous. They also inhibit the production of tears and saliva, explaining the dry mouth and dilated pupils. They can also produce tunnel vision and reduce the range of hearing.

If the hippocampus (memory) and pre-frontal cortex (thinking) areas decide that the fear response is exaggerated, they can dampen down the amygdala's activity. This partly explains why people enjoy watching scary movies; their sensible, thoughtful brain can overpower the primitive parts of the brain's automated fear response.

What you can do that helps

'I am capable of what every other human is capable of. This is one of the great lessons of war and life.'

– Maya Angelou

Our social world requires the discounting of some threats and investing in others.

We revere hindsight (the news) and distrust foresight, which might actually help us. We give lots of attention to fears of things we can't control (airline crashes, tsunamis, earthquakes) and less to things we can control (poor diet, not using phones while driving, car accidents, smoking). We eat junk food and smoke but cancel a holiday because we fear a one in a million terrorist attack.

Who should we fear? If someone doesn't listen to you after you have said no to them on three consecutive occasions, you should consider no longer having them in your life. The people we need around us take our feelings and our boundaries seriously. When someone continually contravenes those feelings and boundaries, you don't want them improved, you want them removed.

Keeping yourself safe

Trust your fear. If you feel apprehensive, concerned or fearful about someone or something, trust that feeling until you can adequately analyse this risk. As Gavin de Becker says, fear is a gift. Our hospital wards are full of people who ignored their concerns that the water was too deep, the bend was a bit sharp to take at that speed or the ladder should be more balanced. We all need to take steps to keep ourselves physically safe. While we live in relatively safe times, cautious observance of risks is wise.

Don't act like a victim. You are not easy prey so don't act like it. Don't wear headphones in dangerous places or while cycling or driving. Always be wary when around drunk or drug-affected people. Think before walking alone in darkened streets. If you feel like you are being followed, it is better to turn around while you are in a well-lit area and look squarely at them.

When having to face an emotional fear – a difficult conversation or talking about potentially touchy subjects such as money or religion – always intend to keep yourself and the people you are with safe. Use the RESOLVE method outlined in the section on Anger to do this.

Forgiveness

Kind, Caring, Peaceful, Calm, Considerate, Gracious, Understanding

Empathic, Relieved, Lightened, Unburdened, Letting go, Being present

'Forgiveness gives us the capacity to make a new start ...
And forgiveness is the grace by which you enable the other
person to get up, and get up with dignity, to begin anew ...
In the act of forgiveness we are declaring our faith in the
future of a relationship and in the capacity of the
wrongdoer to change.'

– Archbishop Desmond Tutu

Anyone who has ever had parents has been forgiven. Anyone who still has some friends has similarly been forgiven. In fact, friendship is an unspoken agreement that 'I'll forgive your flaws, if you'll forgive mine.'

What you may notice

We have all had to forgive someone at some point in our lives. We have all been let down or disappointed by other people. Some of them remain in our lives due to our ability to see that there is more to the person than the hurt they created. If we could never forgive, our pool of friends and family would steadily diminish until we ended up lonely and friendless. When children are behaving at their worst, they need our understanding and forgiveness most of all.

Similarly, we have all been forgiven. We have all upset people, forgotten an important appointment, not returned something on time, hurt another's feelings, said something brash or unwarranted or let down a friend.

Forgiveness is showing mercy to others and ourselves. It is a form of kindness.

What happens

Forgiveness brings freedom. When you forgive someone who hurt you, the person who benefits most is you. It is not weakness. It is not forgetting. It is not acceptance. It is acknowledgement of what has happened and making a clear choice to move on. This can be tough work. It can take years for your heart to soften itself sufficiently to do this. Ultimately, forgiveness allows us not to be defined by the person who has harmed us.

If we hold on to the pain, we often repeat and regurgitate it. In doing so, we poison our lives. This is not to diminish the severity of what happened. This doesn't minimise the dreadful ways you have suffered. Painful pasts are something to heal beyond rather than something to devote your entire future to. If we define our lives by the dreadful things that have happened to us, we wrap our lives in pain.

The pain can fester and develop a life of its own. You no longer need someone else to inflict the pain upon you; you are now doing it repeatedly to yourself. The person suffering most and longest is you. This is not right.

Even worse, the poison can then infect our families. It is tough work for other family members to help someone who suffered greatly and is unable to move on in their lives. None of the issues faced by other family members can ever measure up to the depths of damage they have experienced.

Most family members are not accomplished therapists who could help to heal you. Even if they were, you still couldn't seek their help. This is work that you alone can do.

Forgiveness is an act of self-kindness. It frees you. Through forgiveness we rebuild and renew ourselves.

What you can do that helps

I am indebted to our friend and colleague John Hendry for his thoughts about the feeling of forgiveness. John points out that the easiest way to understand forgiveness is to reverse the syllables. Forgiveness means that you 'give-for' the relationship.

Even if the other person does not see they have caused hurt or pain, even if they show no sign of remorse or regret, it is still worth freeing yourself through forgiveness. Forgiveness is a way of saying to yourself: 'I have been hurt and I deserve to be able to move on. I need to give to myself and to the people who have hurt me so we can all move beyond this. I can restore dignity for myself.'

To repair, we have to give something. We can all put ourselves in the position of having been wronged but that restricts us to the role of being a victim. Seeing ourselves as victims may feel justified in the short term, but if we stay there, we stagnate and never grow beyond the hurts that have been inflicted upon us. Being a victim is not a place of growth.

Forgiveness is not easy. It is a gift to ourselves and others. Emotionally it can take some time before we feel strong enough to forgive.

Our brains often don't differentiate between symbolic acts and real acts. For this reason, writing a forgiveness letter, even if you never send it, is a powerful act of regaining your life. Stating your truth and having the other person hear it, even if it happens only in your imagination, is useful. If you can read it out loud to a trusted friend or a therapist, that can add to the power. Reread the letter out loud until your voice sounds strong and firm.

You might write something like:

'I will never forget the harm that you have caused me. Because of your actions, I have suffered greatly. There are no excuses for what you did. None.

Nevertheless, I am choosing to move on with my life.

My life is greater than the pain you have inflicted upon me.

I recognise that the part of you that hurt me is wounded and hurt itself. This doesn't justify it or excuse it. I do not want to carry the pain inside you that created your actions. For this reason, I am forgiving you and reclaiming my life. It is time to move beyond this.'

Forgiveness allows us to gather together the parts of us that have not been damaged or hurt to heal the parts that have. We become whole again.

Walking on without forgiving

In some instances you will not feel able to forgive. If you choose not to forgive, work with someone so you don't make your pain the centre of your life.

On the next page is a decision tree that you might use in situations where forgiveness may be needed.

Dealing with forgiveness

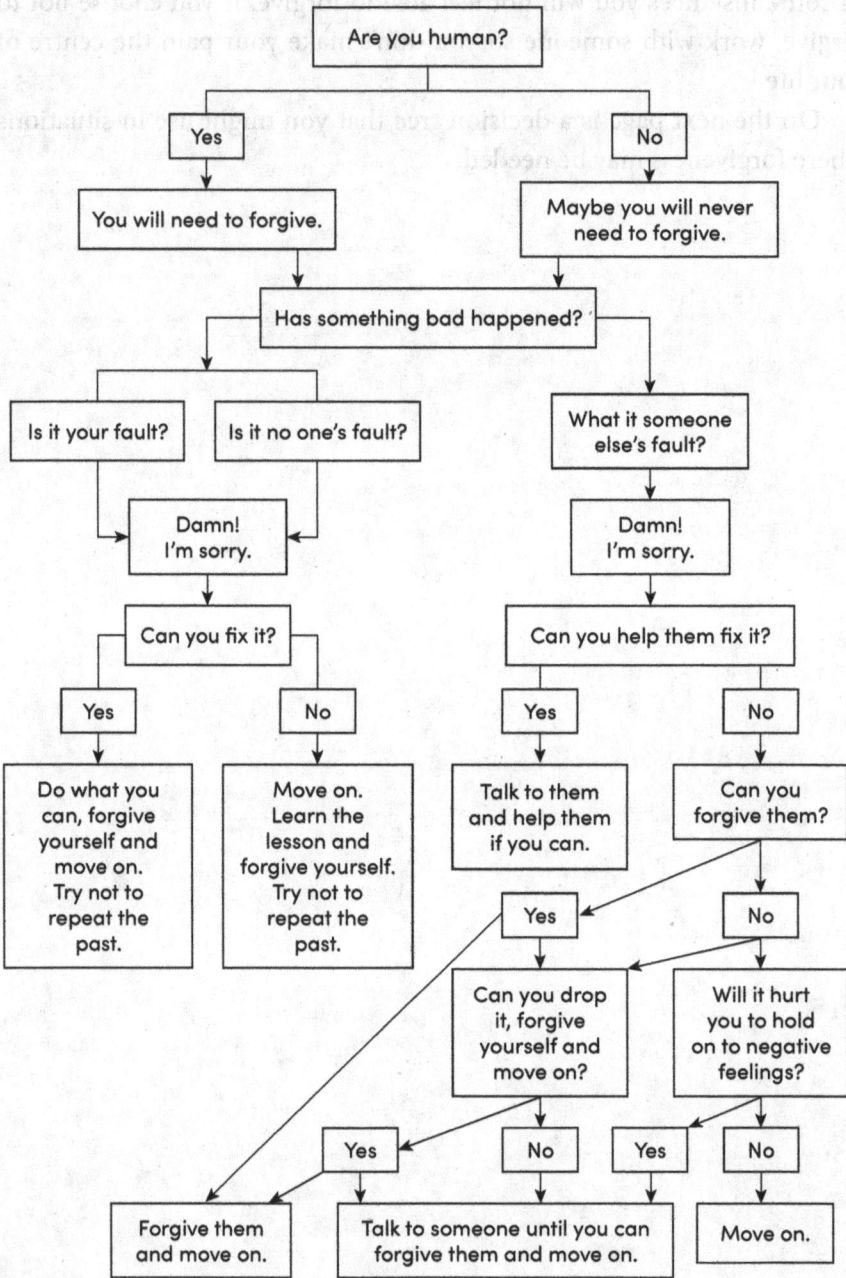

Are you human?

- Yes → **You will need to forgive.**
- No → **Maybe you will never need to forgive.**

Has something bad happened?

Is it your fault? / **Is it no one's fault?** → **Damn! I'm sorry.**

What it someone else's fault? → **Damn! I'm sorry.**

Can you fix it?

- Yes → **Do what you can, forgive yourself and move on. Try not to repeat the past.**
- No → **Move on. Learn the lesson and forgive yourself. Try not to repeat the past.**

Can you help them fix it?

- Yes → **Talk to them and help them if you can.**
- No → **Can you forgive them?**

Can you forgive them?

- Yes → **Can you drop it, forgive yourself and move on?**
- No → **Will it hurt you to hold on to negative feelings?**

Can you drop it, forgive yourself and move on?

- Yes → **Forgive them and move on.**
- No → **Talk to someone until you can forgive them and move on.**

Will it hurt you to hold on to negative feelings?

- Yes → **Talk to someone until you can forgive them and move on.**
- No → **Move on.**

126

Greed and possessiveness

Ambitious, Successful, Go-getter, Desiring, Goal-directed, Acquisitive, Pomposity

Avaricious, Insatiable, Grabbing, Jealous, Unsatisfied, Grasping, Needy

'There must be more to life than having everything.'

– Maurice Sendak

Greed and contentment can never be allies. Greed is a grasping, entitled feeling. If it could speak it would say: 'I deserve it. Give it to me. I want it. I want more. Give me more.'

What you may notice

Greed usually involves attempting to possess more than you need, especially at the expense of others.

A greedy person can only fleetingly experience happiness. The desire to acquire is too strong. Greed is always reminding us that it is not enough to have some things – we need to have more than anyone else. Of course, there are always going to be other people who have more than us.

What happens

Greed stems from our early anxieties that there may not be enough to go around. 'If I don't get in first, I may miss out! Often, in the families of people prone to greed there is a sense that there just wasn't enough love to go around. Greed starts as a perception of love deprivation. This can then generalise to food, alcohol, sex, love, attention, gambling, money or prestige and acceptance.

People who had traumatic upbringings or were abandoned may be prone to have an inner sense of deprivation even when there are adequate supplies. Ideally, we grow up trusting that someone will take care of us and we will be adequately provided for. When this hope is shaken, trust is broken and a better policy might be thought to be grab it now while it's available.

Greed starts as a perception of love deprivation.

Greed makes sharing and collaboration with others difficult. As people stay away from those they perceive to be overly greedy, success becomes more difficult. For this reason, greed is ultimately self-defeating.

Greed is often about possessions. The illusion is that by acquiring lots of possessions, we will be safe. The more we have, the more we have to lose. This is why some very greedy people live behind big walls with razor wire and employ security guards.

Greed has consequences. In some Asian countries, there is a belief that greedy people are destined to become insatiably hungry ghosts in their next lives, with a very large stomach but a tiny mouth.

Of course, people do want things such as food, drink, shelter and security, but if we become too grasping in our wanting, the very things we seek slip through our fingers.

The endlessly wanting brain

We have a good understanding of our endlessly wanting brain but are less clear about the signals that mean someone has had enough.

In the brain there are a number of feedback loops that should indicate that you have had enough. In terms of food, these include glucose, insulin and leptin levels, as well as ghrelin, signifiers of satiety in the stomach. However, all of these signals can be overridden if someone has a panicky sense that there will not be enough in the future.

While the stress hormones and dopamine play their part, it is the pre-frontal cortex that plays a major role in deciding when enough really is enough. Our frontal lobes are the seat of restraint. They help us to develop that inner sense of: 'I wouldn't do that if I was you.'

Learning that your first decision is not always your best decision is usually hard won through life. A series of scalded tongues, scraped knees, sprained ankles and banged elbows in our childhood teaches us that impulses are not always to be trusted.

There is a developmental leap forward in your life when you eventually realise that your first impulse is not always the best. Impulse control requires the development of information processing controls.

What you can do that helps

Become discerning. The world is not full of equal rewards. Some things are more valued by you than others. Not every issue is yours to take on. Not every quest is yours to pursue. Not every person will be influenced by your opinion.

Define 'enough'

Ask yourself the following questions:

- What is success to you?
- How much money is enough?
- How much fame?
- How much acknowledgement?

These are difficult questions to answer but unless you at least have a go at them, you can be on an endless unsatisfying pursuit for more.

Big pie versus little pie thinking

Big pie thinkers act as if there is enough pie to go around for everyone. Little pie thinkers believe there is only so much pie to go around and if they don't get in and get a piece now they will miss out.

If you take on a little-pie approach to the world, you are always on guard for people who might take advantage of you or disrespect you. Big pie thinkers are more able to be generous, open, sharing and trusting. Aim to be a big pie thinker.

Resisting temptation

Controlling our impulses is something we get better at as we mature. However, our grip on it is fickle at times and seems to diminish as the day wears on. What feels like a rock-solid resolution in the bright morning sunlight becomes an idea by mid-afternoon and by evening often shrinks to a hint, a suggestion or a mere possibility.

When psychologist Walter Mischel offered children two marshmallows, he really started something. Mischel had designed a test that involved a series of children sitting alone in a room with two marshmallows. The children were told that if they ate a marshmallow while he was out of the room then they wouldn't get the other one. But if the children waited until he came back before eating the first marshmallow, they could then have both marshmallows. Only 30 per cent of the children in his study were able to resist the first marshmallow.

The longer children were able to wait at four or five years of age, the higher their school results. They also had better social and cognitive function in the teen years. As adolescents, they exhibited more self-control, were less distractible, more intelligent, self-reliant and confident, and trusted their own judgment. The children who were able to resist immediate temptation were more resilient in times of stress.

Not grabbing that first marshmallow and stuffing it into their mouths was designed to test the children's levels of self-control. It demonstrated that the ability not to do the first thing that comes into your mind was a powerful predictor of success in life.

Developing impulse control

Having no impulse control would be like taking an overly curious monkey into a fine glassware shop while it is wearing a blindfold. You can't really plan anything; you can only wait and react to what happens.

Similarly, we all have greedy impulses from time to time and need to develop skills to restrain ourselves. Controlling our first impulses gives us a chance to reconsider and redirect our attention and our actions. This ability enables us to stay on task and protects us from blundering onwards and sometimes making fools of ourselves. Impulse control is our inner stop/start sign.

Grief

Reconciled, Acceptance, Reverence, Honour, Healing, Acceptance

Lost, Stricken, Bereft, Shattered, Empty, Denial, Anger, Bargaining, Depression, Gutted

My heart is heavy-laden now; I sit
Burning my dreams away beside the fire:
For death has made me wise and bitter and strong;
And I am rich in all I have lost.'

– Siegfried Sassoon

And I am rich in all I have lost. When Siegfried Sassoon wrote those lines at the end of World War I it must have been with a weary acceptance of the gift that life had bestowed upon him.

What you may notice

Grief slams into our being like a freight train. It enters every pore and permeates our every fibre, every molecule. There is an appalling sense that life has emptied irrevocably.

Grief is the price we pay for loving. We grieve for the people, animals or things we have loved. We can also grieve for parts of ourselves. Often there is an inner death as well as the outer death. Grief can depress the immune system.

If we don't learn to respect grief and take the time to allow its lessons to slowly unveil themselves, we may become embittered and feel incomplete.

Unsettled grief echoes and reverberates down the generations. This is why ambivalent grief, or grief where you have mixed feelings about the loss, can be so damaging and set people on a course for prolonged depression. The mixed feelings involved can tear people apart.

The original meaning of suffering was 'to allow'. We need to allow grief to happen. Observe it. Most of us want to rush people through their grief and get uncomfortable if we think someone is grieving too long or too extravagantly. Shah Jahan built the Taj Mahal when his beloved wife Mumtaz Mahal died giving birth. The family didn't take it quite so well when Shah Jahan announced he was going to create another Taj on the other side of the river – this time in black – and promptly put him under house arrest.

We have a long history of impatience with grief. We also have a sense that we alone experience grief. It is often proprietorial in nature, and can cause devastating battles in all too many families following a death. Who is grieving the most? Whose grief is the most important?

Let's patiently and quietly consider this inevitable human emotion and bear in mind Maurice Sendak and Ruth Krauss's advice: that everybody should be quiet near a little stream and listen.

What happens

My wise mentor Peter O'Connor, also a psychologist who specialises in mythology, speaks eloquently of the inner journey of grief. As we grieve for others we have lost we get a chance to revisit and reconsider the parts of ourselves that have also been lost.

The parts that died young

Within us all there are ideas and dreams that died young. Hopes and ambitions that were stifled through criticism, disapproval or lack of opportunity; stillborn possibilities that have stayed within us.

Do these aspects of ourselves that died young need to be re-buried or resurrected? This is a question all of us need to reflect upon.

The parts that died violently

There are aspects of ourselves that, through denigration, guilt, broken hearts and betrayal, have been killed off violently. As such they are not dealt with properly and tend to resurface when we least expect it. Although we may resolve vehemently to never ever do a particular thing again, in doing so we curse ourselves to do precisely that. We cover up past guilt, rush into deciding what we are not and destine ourselves to repeat the very thing that caused us guilt in the first place.

Grief has an if-only quality to it. If only they were still here. If only that didn't happen. This can be comforting and stifling at the same time.

There are times when we need to identify the corpse of our own dreams. We need to look and see what has died within us. What is it that we need to bury in order to embrace a new form of life?

To achieve this we need to sit through the dark night of the soul, endure confusion, reflect and not rush towards premature certainty. All things we, as humans, hate doing!

Those who hadn't been buried properly

There are also aspects of ourselves that need to be downsized, if not killed off and buried entirely. We have outgrown some aspects of ourselves and need to respectfully and properly bury them once and for all. This is the process of maturing and it requires patient reflection and awareness.

As we live in a world that has little patience for uncertainty, an intolerance for indecision and an aversion to reflective thinking, many people are haunted and stunted by the restless dead within themselves. They continue to battle with parts of themselves that should have been buried long ago; they fantasise about re-acquainting themselves with the parts that died violently through disapproval and yearn for the fulfilment offered by parts of their lives that died young.

So grief is painful. It is also part of life. But by sitting with it, feeling it, it has great lessons to teach us all. This is why I began with Siegfried Sassoon's line.

Physical signs of grief

- decreased immune functioning
- distractibility
- ruminative sadness
- tiredness
- pain sensitivity increases
- inability to think clearly
- shock
- sleep disturbance
- anxiety.

What you can do that helps

Leonard Cohen expressed a similar thought to Sassoon when he wrote in his song 'Anthem', 'There is a crack, a crack in everything, that's how the light gets in.'

An excellent analogy for grief was written by a wise elderly man on Reddit after someone uploaded a post, asking: 'My friend just died. I don't know what to do.' The man responded:

I'm old. What that means is that I've survived and a lot of people I've known and loved did not … I wish I could say you get used to people dying. I never did. I never want to. It tears a hole in me whenever somebody I love dies, no matter the circumstances. But I don't want it to not matter. I don't want it to be something that just passes.

My scars are a testament to the love and the relationship that I had with that person. And if the scar is deep, so was the love. My scars are a testament that I can love deeply and live deeply and be cut, or even gouged, and that I can heal and continue to love and continue to live.

And the scar tissue is stronger than the original flesh ever was. Scars are a testament to life. Scars are only ugly to people who can't see.

As for grief you'll find it comes in waves. When the ship is first wrecked, you're drowning with wreckage all around you. Everything floating around you reminds you of the beauty and the magnificence of the ship that was and is no more. And all you can do is float. You find some piece of wreckage and you hang on for a while. Maybe it's a physical thing. Maybe it's a happy memory and a photograph. Maybe it is a person who is still floating. For a while, all you can do is float, stay alive.

In the beginning the waves are 100 feet tall and crash over you without mercy. They come 10 seconds apart and don't even give you time to catch your breath. All you can do is hang on and float. After a while, maybe weeks, maybe months and it's different for everyone, you find the waves are only 80 feet high or 50 feet high and while they still come, they are further apart. You can see them coming – an anniversary, Christmas. You can see them coming and prepare yourself and when it washes over you know you will come out the other side – soaking wet sputtering still hanging to some piece of wreckage but you'll come through.

Take it from an old man, the waves never stop coming and somehow you don't really want them to but you learn that you'll survive those and other waves will come. And you'll survive those too. If you're lucky, you'll have lots of waves from lots of loves and lots of shipwrecks.

Some grief is too big to ever recover from. You will be changed forever by it. It indelibly marks your life. Take the time with it you need but don't be afraid or feel guilty to live with it and around it at the same time. You can grieve and also live.

When you are broken-hearted, use your broken heart to open up your life. Slowly, gently and as gradually as you need, allow wholeheartedness to form out of your broken heart.

The grieving brain

When you are grieving, your brain function takes a hit. Emotional regulation, memory, multi-tasking, organisation and the ability to learn all suffer. During grief, a flood of neurochemicals and hormones, such as adrenaline and cortisol, are continually being released. This not only makes you feel extra sad and despondent but has an affect on your immune system, making you susceptible to getting sick.

The longer your grief goes on, the more the thinking part of your brain becomes affected and the less likely you will be able to concentrate and make good decisions. This is why so many of us choose to self-medicate with drugs or alcohol in times of extreme stress or grief. Our decision-making ability has been compromised by the flood of stress hormones in our system.

Recovering successfully from grief has an upside: it increases your inner resilience and your stress limits. You will cope better next time you are in the same situation.

Happiness

Pleasure, Rejoicing, Amusement, Relief, Pride, Ecstasy, Joy, Glee, Delight, Bliss

Compassion, Wonder, Enthusiasm, Elation, Hopeful, Thrilled, Euphoric, Excitement

'I felt once more how simple and frugal a thing is happiness:
a glass of wine, a roast chestnut, a wretched little brazier, the
sound of the sea. Nothing else.'

– Nikos Kazantzakis, *Zorba the Greek*

Happiness is a fickle friend. It shows up at the oddest moments and just when you are lured into relying on it, it vanishes. Whenever some of our needs are met, we immediately start wishing for more.

What you may notice

Seeking happiness can make you miserable.

'I have reigned more than fifty years in victory and peace,' the great caliph Abdul Rahim once remarked. 'During this time I have been beloved by my people, dreaded by my enemies, and respected by my allies. Riches and honours, power and pleasure have all been at my beck and call, nor has any earthly pleasure been missing to complete my sense of perfect bliss. In this situation I have diligently numbered the days of pure and genuine happiness that have fallen to my lot. They number fourteen.'

In 2000 when the torch was being relayed around Australia before the Sydney Olympics, it arrived in the town of Bendigo and into the hands of the oldest relay runner, Jack Lockett. Jack was 109 years old at the time and completed his part of the relay watched by his four children, the youngest of whom was John, a sprightly spring chicken aged only 85.

After his run, Jack was asked about his life and he said, 'Well, in my life I've had my worries but I decided not to worry about them.'

I wonder who you would prefer to be more like? Abdul Rahim or Jack Lockett? My money is on Jack.

What happens

Happiness is difficult to achieve, partly because the universe was not designed with the comfort of human beings in mind. The world does not provide happiness. Happiness is created by people and those people are us.

If you are seeking happiness, you are seeking misery. The things that make us happy can also make us unhappy. You get a great job then the stress makes you ill. You become famous then you can't go out in the street. This doesn't mean you can't or shouldn't pursue your goals, but don't expect them to make you happy. Happiness is alignment with the present moment.

Happiness was once thought of as the most dangerous emotion because we chase after it and sell our souls for it.

Contrary to what most of us believe, happiness is not mostly associated with passive, relaxing times. We think that whiling away the hours beside a pool at a resort, a drink in one hand and an object of desire in the other, should be our happiest moments.

While I am personally prepared to sacrifice myself to undertake further research in this area, it does appear that our happiest times aren't when we are passively relaxing but when we are unselfconsciously absorbed in a mindful challenge.

A mindful challenge can be any activity that immerses us in the experience so much that we forget about who we are, and what our daily concerns are. Experiences that cause us to look up and think, 'Where did the time go?' People often describe this state of being immersed in the experience as flow.

These activities are ones where we have some skills to meet demands and the relationship between the challenge and the skills needed is balanced. If the challenge is too great, we experience anxiety. If the challenge is too low we become bored.

People report many activities that they engage in to develop a sense of flow: sport, games, socialising, drawing, art, music, reading, gardening, fishing, walking, playing with children or pets, even work.

Physical signs of happiness

- smiling, laughter
- open face
- hugging people
- jumping up and down
- enthusiastic voice
- openness and expansiveness
- talkative, pupils dilated.

The distinctive feature of these activities is that typically they involve the person setting their own goals and providing their own rewards. It is by engaging in these activities that they free themselves from needing to wait for the world to provide challenges and rewards. However, even the sense of flow is fleeting, so how do we go about creating enduring happiness?

What you can do that helps

All of our knowledge about happiness shows us that our happiest times are not about indulging ourselves. Happiness comes from doing things that are meaningful and benefit others.

For parents who want their children to be happy, teach them about how to make a contribution to their relationships and in their future working life.

One of the most common misguided things parents say of their children is, 'I just want them to be happy.' Given that happiness is a topsy-turvy unpredictable beast, this is a mission bound for intermittent failure. Firstly, it sends the wrong message: 'If you're not happy, something must be wrong.' This draws a false link between the absence of happiness and some personal deficiency within the child or inadequacy in the quality of their parenting. Secondly, it is not achievable as a consistent state of being. Life has its slings and arrows. Parents would do better to focus on helping their children have a strong sense of identity and a sense of being loved and belonging.

While happiness may be fleeting and unreliable, here are some sure-fire ways to increase your chances of creating it.

Don't wait to see if you are having a good time

Instead of going to places and seeing if it is fun, decide in advance to have fun regardless of the circumstances. Enjoy the day regardless of the weather. Make the most of the occasion regardless of the company.

Go outside and play

You were told to do this as a kid and I'm telling you to do it again: play more. Go for walks, throw a dog a stick, skip, sing loudly or imagine yourself to be a spy passing through enemy territory. Whatever does it for you. Make a promise to play more.

Develop deep friendships

Your friends are your true wealth. Value them and see them regularly. Let them know how important they are to you. Most people only have two close friends, so don't fool yourself into believing you are less popular than most people.

Increase the closeness of extended family

Keeping in close contact with your family gives you a support base for difficult times and also strengthens your sense of where you came from. Feeling you belong in a family is a powerful way of being happy.

Play to your strengths

Have a long, hard look at yourself. What are you good at? Go to www.mylearningstrengths.com and find out your learning strengths. Make a commitment to develop your skills, talents and abilities as much as you can. If you don't develop your own unique talents, the world misses out.

Seek out groups that value what you have to offer

Finding the niche where your abilities are valued is the basis of success.

Avoid social groups where your unique attributes are not valued

Not everyone is going to like you or think you could amount to much. Get used to it. Accept that it is so, and then get out of their way.

Live in the dreamtime

Find and follow your passions. Dream big dreams and make a promise to yourself to live a wonderful life.

Laugh a lot more

Find people, shows, books, movies and situations that make you laugh and surround yourself with them.

Hate

Anger, Angst, Social, Action, Empowerment, Bonding

Vengeful, Obsessed, Fixated, Loathing

'Stronger than lover's love is lover's hate.
Incurable, in each,
the wounds they make.'

– Euripides, *Medea*

'Next time I'll find a woman I hate and give her a house,' Rod Stewart lamented after one of his divorces.

People are a fickle, ambivalent lot. If someone can satisfy us, they can also frustrate us; and if someone can frustrate us, we always believe that they can satisfy us. Wherever we hate, we love; whatever we love, we hate.

What you may notice

Hate is powerful and hate is generous. When we love someone we usually want exclusive rights; when we hate someone we want everyone to join in.

Teaching other people to hate what you hate is psychologically damaging. Forming a community of hate may shore up your own view but it won't help you.

Emotions work best when they flow through us and don't linger. Hate doesn't flow, it stagnates. It clings parasitically to the psyche. As Oscar Wilde observed, 'Hate destroys everything around it, except itself.'

People cling to hate because they know if they relinquish it they will have to deal with the pain.

141

Physical signs of hate

- pupils constrict
- fixed stare or glaring
- hands clenching into fists
- asymmetrical nose wrinkling.

What happens

Love and hate appear to be opposite feelings but they are actually linked as they involve some of the same neural circuitry. In 2008, Professor Semir Zeki of University College London performed brain scans on volunteers who were shown pictures of people they hated. The results showed that the parts of the brain that were activated during the photo viewing were the putamen and insula. These are the areas of the brain that are activated by the emotions of romantic love, as well as disgust.

Parts of the cerebral cortex, associated with reasoning and judgment, become deactivated during love but only become slightly deactivated during feelings of hate. That means, for the most part, the brain is still using its best judgment when you feel hatred!

Love can become a fertile ground for the emergence of hate. If the intensity and intimacy of love sours, feelings of hate may emerge. In these circumstances, hate serves as a channel of communication.

Love can be extremely dangerous. As we know, people can commit the most heinous crimes in the name of love. People have murdered their families and killed themselves, preferring death to the pain of rejection.

As intense an emotion as love is, so is hate.

What you can do that helps

When we hate something or someone we can't seem to let it go. Hate is the strongest attachment – stronger than love and stronger than blood. When we dislike someone we walk away. When we fear someone we run away. But when we hate someone we attach ourselves to the feeling.

When we hate someone we like to think we are nothing like them. However, hate means we focus all of our rage and disgust on that person and depend on them to live out parts of our shadow; the parts of ourselves we don't like to admit to.

Hatred says more about us than it does about who or what we hate. The object of hate is actually a reflection of the lost and despised parts of our own psyche. When we hate it is a signal: here are the things I can't live with yet here is where I have lost my way. Missing the lesson of our hate can have a number of consequences to our growth and development as a human.

Choosing not to hate

Hate can make our emotions feel congealed or stuck, especially if we have been hurt or mistreated. Hate is a tempting way to reintegrate ourselves after we have been hurt. Some people can make vengeance and hate a central mission of their lives. The only problem is that false integration stifles growth. Some of the people who are most afflicted by hate spend their lives bashing the pain out of themselves. You may sometimes see this in angry young men.

You may never recover from the dreadful hurts that have been done to you. Nevertheless, you do get a choice on how to respond. You can take all the hurt that has been directed at you and let it fill your life. Be aware though that the act of seeking vengeance and revenge will, in one way or another, grind its way into your heart.

Alternatively, you can choose not to waste your life on hate towards another person and choose kindness towards yourself instead. This may be the toughest choice you will ever make. Deciding that you are worth more than the pain that has been inflicted upon you is a life-preserving decision. And it is a decision that only you can make – and only you can act on. You can't be convinced by someone else to stop hating someone. You have to feel it yourself.

> **Choosing kindness towards yourself may be the toughest choice you will ever make.**

Generally, choosing kindness is not a gradual decision, where you mount enough evidence to convince yourself to recover enough to shift towards kindness. It is a flip. You have to give up one feeling to take up another. Mixed feelings don't work well here. It is a decision that only you can make for yourself. Work with someone by all means to prepare yourself, but ultimately, it is your decision to make.

Choosing kindness instead of hate means you have made the choice to start living with purpose. It is a chance to stop asking yourself, 'Why did this happen?' and start asking yourself, 'How can I make a better future?' It is a chance to focus on your own growth, and not the stagnation of personal development that hate generates.

Hate and the brain

Our insular cortex, the part of our brain related to disgust, also plays a role in hate. As author Robert Sapolsky points out, because we are able to think symbolically and metaphorically, we can have a sense of moral disgust or hate for specific people, actions or ideologies, as well as for physical and tangible things like rotten fruit or spoiled meat.

Our brains try to create patterns. These patterns give us shortcuts to predicting the future. (Read: big survival value.) However, our brains can't differentiate well between metaphors and real experiences. This means the context of when and where we experience something – how a room smells, whether we are holding a warm or cold drink, what mood we happen to be in at a certain time – has a lot of influence on whether we hate something. Associating a group of people with something our brain perceives as disgusting often results in hatred.

This not only helps to explain racism (see the discussion of us-and-them thinking on page 94), but also why people who have had chemotherapy often hate the smell of hospitals.

Hurt and heartbreak

Vulnerable, Humble, Grounded, Saddened, Fragile

Complaining, Bitter, Rejected, Fury, Despising, Contemptuous, Emotionally bruised

When the heart
is cut or cracked or broken
Do not clutch it
Let the wound lie open

Let the wind
From the good old sea blow in
To bathe the wound with salt
And let it sting

Let a stray dog lick it
Let a bird lean in the hole and sing
A simple song like a tiny bell
And let it ring.

– Michael Leunig, 'When the heart'

If we don't transform pain, we transmit it. It can echo and reverberate down the generations.

When we are hurt we are like a migratory bird returning for the spring to find the nest that we left intact is scattered and broken. Our dreams have been shattered, our hopes have been dashed, our trust has been abused.

What you may notice

Suffering and feeling hurt are feelings none of us seek out. They are also feelings none of us can avoid. We feel hurt because we love and care.

145

Robots and machines don't feel hurt. Feeling hurt is understandable and unavoidable and is a sign we need to recover our sense of self.

What happens

Heartbreak is something we all hope we can avoid, something to guard against, a dark pit to be carefully circumvented. However, the risk of loving deeply is heartbreak. This is tough. Heartbreak ain't for sissies.

Heartbreak is how we mature; yet we use the word heartbreak as if it only occurs when things have gone wrong: an unrequited love, a shattered dream, a child lost before their time. Heartbreak can actually be the start of growth if you let it.

Heartbreak asks us not to look for an alternative path because there is no alternative path. It is a deeper introduction to what we love and have loved, an inescapable and often beautiful question, something or someone who has been with us all along, asking us to be ready for the last letting go. In this way it intertwines with grief.

What you can do that helps

One way to recover from heartbreak and hurt is to mentally sit beside these feelings as you might beside a close friend in need of comfort. Perhaps you can feel their tenderness and sadness. Perhaps you can relate to their deep sense of disappointment and desolation. Things have not turned out as planned. Love has become a wound.

Just sit with the hurt. Let it be there. You can be deeply, profoundly sad without being depressed. Let it speak its experience but don't allow it to take up the entire conversation. Acknowledge the hurt and the not-hurt parts of yourself. Don't try to shift or cure your sense of hurt. It is an appropriate feeling after all that has happened.

Try not to let your hurt bubble its way into anger. While anger can alleviate hurt briefly, in the end, it solves nothing. Anger and blame just lead back to more hurt.

Hurt feelings can also infiltrate and spoil the best of relationships. Left to fester, hurt can turn into bitterness, dislike and resentment. It can entrench itself and divide your heart.

To sit and gently accept your own deep sense of hurt will strengthen your recognition of hurt.

Sitting with hurt eventually takes us towards compassion, for ourselves and for others. It will also strengthen your recognition of hurt. If you feel hurt it is likely that others do too, and being able to sense that will enable you to extend compassion towards them.

As you sit beside your own hurt, use it to forge your resolve. Use it to gather the compassion and the energy to build a better life. You can think on the following suggestions as you are sitting and use them to help you find your way back into the world.

Give up influencing outcomes

No persuasion, no coercion, no consequences, no influence. For the time being, let the situation be what the situation is. Let the person be who the person is.

Act for the good of others

Use your feelings of hurt to act for the good of others. While you have been embroiled in dramas, some important people in your life may have been neglected. If there is someone you know who is lonely, visit them. If someone needs a compliment, make it. Walk with people on their journeys.

Be true to your word

Be the person you intend to be, now. Do what you say you will do. In the heat of disputes your other commitments can fall by the wayside. This is understandable but also diminishes your reputation. If there are people who have been let down by you while you dealt with your intense feelings, now might be a good time to make it up to them.

Avoid criticism

Give it up. Decide to make no negative comments about anyone. As hard as it seems, practise forgiveness.

Be kind

No one likes feeling hurt but it does help us to relate to how many people feel much of the time. Hurt helps us to feel grounded and humble.

Most of the people you meet are going through a fairly tough time, so remember to be kind.

Use the hurt you feel to rebuild the quality relationships in your life.

Love and the brain

Love is like an addiction. The feeling of love is activated in the caudate nucleus by a flood of dopamine. The caudate nucleus is associated with motivation or the reward system.

Recovering from a break-up is like overcoming a long-term drug addiction, with all of the erratic behaviour and feelings that can involve. Take your time when recovering from hurt and heartbreak

Identity and belonging

Settled, Connected, Self-assured, Sense of purpose and meaning

Accepted, Valued, Appreciated, Self-aware

'A deep sense of belonging is an irreducible need of all people.'

– Brene Brown

A sense of belonging is our most powerful antidote to violence, drug abuse, suicide and self-harm in our society. Whether we are a newborn baby or the toughest leader of a gang, we all seek to belong. Extroverts may find it in a web of social connections, introverts in quiet intimacy. We all seek to belong somewhere and to something.

Compassion and love are our oldest medicines. If you add hope and a sense of belonging to these two, we have the four most powerful ingredients of healing.

Each ingredient alone may not cure a case of the flu but, together, they will help you resist disease, lower stress, lower blood pressure, avoid a heart attack, protect against depression, increase academic results and longevity, and live a happier life.

The quest of many people's lives is often to try to answer two questions:

1. Who am I?
2. Where do I belong?

Resolving these questions and feeling a sense of who you are and where and how you belong really helps people to settle into themselves. It also goes a long way in creating a meaningful life. The process of self-discovery is worth understanding as we all go through setbacks and steps forward in understanding ourselves.

What you may notice

Canadian psychologist James Marcia found that people attempt to answer the questions of who they are and where they belong using two main dimensions – exploration and commitment.

This means that during your adolescence you may well try a whole lot of different things and ideas out, such as religion, politics, role models, beliefs and ways of thinking, before discarding some of them while committing to others. These go on to form the basis of your identity.

During the process of exploration, several things may happen which can affect the overall result of who you end up being.

Diffusion/Confusion

You might be the type of person who is hesitant and uncertain about which direction to take in life. You might be confused and anxious about who you are. And your anxiety will be compounded by the fact that you feel you should know by now!

Your fears and worries can make you vulnerable to falling prey to fads, cults, the influence of role models (both positive and negative), and finding yourself in unsafe work places.

As you feel beset with worry about what to do, you generally don't do anything. This can be temporary, as when faced with a life transition of some sort, or if it becomes an ongoing state then it is more a sort of paralysis by indecision and fear.

Foreclosure/Shut down

This is when you feel, 'This is the best I can be' and there is no desire or enthusiasm for improvement. Some people get so stuck in this state that they lack any vision to see their way forward. Passions that once burned fiercely, sputter. Dreams are pared back. You may feel you have invested so much in viewing yourself in a particular way that you lack the capacity to change.

Moratorium/Wait and see

This can be the healthiest position. It is a time of high exploration without feeling the need to commit to any specific course of action. It can be a time of discovery.

Moratorium centres around the idea 'I'm not quite sure who I am so I'll hang out and wait and see who shows up.' This often accompanies contentment and exploration of life for the twenty-something-year-old.

While this state can often be seen as 'wasting time' by other people, tolerating uncertainty pays great dividends. Delaying the decision about the type of person you are and exploring how life works can set up your future. Experimenting and exploring opportunities now broadens your horizons for the years to come. The more colours you accumulate on your palette, the more vivid your canvas will be.

Achievement/Life ready

At this stage you might have found a positive identity through being successful. At some stage in your childhood or adolescence someone said to you: 'You are good at this!' Whatever 'this' is, you might think: 'If people think I'm good at this, I'll do this.' Usually there are lots of rewards for doing 'this'. You gain social approval. You often get to be at the right end of the school hall on speech night.

While this is generally positive, it can also trap you into only doing those activities that you are successful at. Without consciously knowing it, you place limits on yourself. These are the people who often tumble back into my therapy rooms in their late forties or early fifties, realising that they were so busy climbing their one ladder, they didn't see that they had placed it against the wrong wall to begin with.

Of course, life is complex and you may be in more than one of these states in different aspects and stages of your life. For example, you could feel settled and content in your relationships (Achievement) but feel trapped in your job with no way out (Foreclosure) and personally feel ready to explore different ways of living your life (Moratorium).

Over the page is a table showing identity formation based on percentages of school leavers that demonstrates how rare it is to leave school fully ready for life.

Identity Formation

Exploration

Low	High

Diffusion/confusion (21%)	Moratorium/wait and see (21%)
No exploration, no commitments	*Exploration of alternatives before committing*
Can be carefree or confused	Stable self-esteem
If confused may ruminate	Non-conformist
Becomes disorganised under stress	High level of moral thinking
Lower level of moral thinking	Cognitive level may not match results
Lower level of relationships	
Often marked difference with same-sex parent who they feel they can neither emulate nor please	May shift from harsh self-condemnation to lax permissiveness
No sense of having choice	Differentiating from parents
	May be insecure in attachment
	Exploring choices
	Anxious
Foreclosure/shut down (40%)	**Achievement/life ready (16%)**
Commitment without exploration	*Commitment after exploring alternatives*
Inflexible, close-minded	Non-conforming to group pressure
Can agree superficially or resist stubbornly	Think effectively under stress
May give the appearance but not the reality of closeness	Higher levels of moral reasoning
More reliant on others	Better relationships
Either secure or insecure	More self-reliant
May conform to the expectations of others	Low level of reconsideration
Fearful, avoidant	Come from families where differences among members are accepted
	Capable of secure attachment
	Perfectionism

Commitment (Low → High, vertical axis)

What happens

A common pattern is Moratorium/Achievement/Moratorium/Achievement (MAMA) where people alternate between times of moratorium and times of achievement. This is an adaptive trying-out of different and new options before re-evaluating whether those possibilities are worth committing to.

A more limiting cycle is Diffusion/Foreclosure/Diffusion/Foreclosure (DFDF) where a person summons up enough courage to try something, encounters a setback and concludes they are not up to it.

What you can do that helps

Like most people, your life has been a combination of accomplishments and setbacks. The setbacks may be associated with feelings of shame/remorse/disappointment/failure. Even though you may find this hard to admit, our setbacks take up more mental real estate than our successes. It is easy to dismiss any success we have had as a product of lucky circumstances while deeply suspecting that our setbacks are a true reflection of our own flaws and inadequacy.

There are a number of things you can do to rectify this way of thinking:

1. Retell your life story as an unremitting list of failures, disappointments and bad outcomes. Then retell your life story as a highlights reel of your best moments and your finest accomplishments. Now become your own best friend and be the supporter you need to create the next phase of your life.

2. Go to www.mylearningstrengths.com and analyse your own pattern of learning strengths. An understanding of your strengths will help you to determine the next phase of your life.

3. Decide to base your future on the best aspects of your past rather than the worst.

4. Construct a life big enough to live in. Be devoted to your own creativity. Inspiration rarely comes without time and focus. Just as a garden needs water, ideas need interest and contemplation. Ideas regarded with interest, grow and develop. Those ignored or treated

with contempt shrivel and die. We can be too fast to judge and too busy to develop.

To accomplish this we need to develop an idea-capturing device. Inspirations are slippery and unless taken hold of and recorded, they can vanish.

We also need to learn how to pay close attention to dreams and sudden intuitions. Your unconscious is a faithful, diligent helper. Trust it with problems to solve and it will very often start giving you answers.

It is also great to develop crazy wisdom where you put together two or more seemingly incompatible ideas in nonsensical ways. Some combinations may be funny or weird, but by doing this we loosen up the fibres of imagination in our minds.

Many great ideas and dreams are never born at all as people rail against thought.

We can carry scar tissue from the wounds of childhood. These are the knots that block creativity and performance. It could have been a critical comment about something you tried (eg singing, dancing, art, cooking, storytelling) or a doubtful stance someone took towards your capacities. Original thinkers are often seen as slow by others.

Author Virginia Woolf speaks to the value of journalling in granting us unfiltered access to the rough gems of our own minds, ordinarily dismissed by the self-censorship of formal writing, when she says, 'The habit of writing thus for my own eye only is good practice. It loosens the ligaments. Never mind the misses and the stumbles.'

5. Become a seeker. Our sources of fascination and belonging vary. Some people find them in people, some in music, others in trains and yet others in obscure species of birds. The target of your curiosity is not as important as just being curious.

    Become more interested in what you don't know than in the things you do know. Wonder and curiosity mean you don't have the answer before you ask the question.

    Walt Disney had three rooms in which he used to come up with creative thoughts. In the first he was a dreamer combining new ideas. In the second, he was a realist looking at the shortcomings of an idea. In the third room he was a critic who would consider if the idea had entertainment value and whether it could be done even better.

Edward de Bono, who originated the term lateral thinking, developed a system of thinking using six different-coloured hats: red for feelings; black for cautions; yellow for benefits; green for creativity; white for facts; and blue for process.

The process of creativity is one of spark and sift. Sparking new ideas is exciting but sifting and revealing the great ideas from the not-so-great may be even more important.

6. Notice the things that irritate you and other people. About 50 years ago, IKEA employee Gillis Lungren had a problem. He was trying to fit a table into the boot of his car. By taking the legs off the table and lying it flat in the boot he found it fitted. In doing so, he inadvertently invented the flat packaging used by IKEA.

7. Assume there is a missed opportunity, because there usually is.

8. In 1995, Pierre Omiday was considering how auctions worked and combined it with the internet to create eBay. What object is as unimaginable as the internet was in 1980?

A problem is an opportunity in drag.

– Paul Hawken

Revisioning your life

There are times when we need to take some time to recharge and refresh. Often in the process we discover new aspects of ourselves. If you can, take some time away from the urgent demands that occupy you and try to write a preferred future for yourself. This will be useful at many different times of life but especially if you have recently experienced a major change or transition.

Jealousy

Suspiciousness, Wary, Clinging, Guarded, Cautious, Distrusting, Watchful

Competitive, Envious, Greedy, Petty, Possessive, Controlling, Rivalrous, Obsessed

'The jealous are troublesome to others,
but a torment to themselves.'

– William Penn

Jealousy is an intense, fiery feeling we can experience towards rivals for things we desire, such as love or ambition. Jealousy is often really a fear of loss. Someone is going to rob you of someone or something.

Jealousy never ends well. The fairytale *Snow White and the Seven Dwarfs* is a classic story of jealousy. The rivalry between Snow White and her stepmother as to who is the fairest in all the land shows the destructive nature of jealousy where Snow White ends up being the housekeeper for seven vertically challenged gentlemen with personality disorders. The stepmother fares even worse; in the traditional version by the Brothers Grimm, she is forced to don red-hot iron slippers and dance until she drops dead.

In the fairytale the stepmother fears the loss of beauty and desirability and asks the well-known question of her magic mirror:

'Mirror, Mirror on the wall
Am I most beautiful of all?'

To her surprise, the mirror replies:

'Fair queen thou art the fairest here,
But at the palace, now,
The bride will prove a thousand times
More beautiful than thou.'

The jealous stepmother becomes consumed by being displaced by someone more beautiful, illustrating one of the common aspects of jealousy: anticipating loss or abandonment before it has occurred. The stepmother goes on to make three attempts on Snow White's life. On the third attempt, she appears to succeed by using a poisoned apple, only to have Snow White saved by a dashing young prince. Talk about gnashing your teeth with jealousy! The stepmother's preoccupation with Snow White comes at a great expense to herself as she is punished to her death.

While jealousy is dangerous by itself, if left unchecked it can grow into stalking, possessiveness or predatory behaviour and relationship violence.

Physical signs of jealousy

- fast heart rate
- choking sensation
- muscles tensing, especially the jaw
- teeth clenching
- pupils constricting
- spouting demeaning or belittling comments about other people.

What you may notice

We live in a competitive world that promotes jealousy through marketing. We exist in an age where if someone gets something good, someone else feels they have been denied. This is promoted by an inequity of distribution.

Of course, both jealousy and envy are preoccupations with comparison and direct your energy towards other people and prizes. Social media can make some people particularly jealous. As they compare lives, they think everyone else's looks so much better than their own. They fear losing their own reputation by comparison. One young woman even confessed in my therapy session to being jealous of her own social media profile based on the idea that it was so much better than her real life.

Feeling jealous means we need to take care of and love ourselves a bit more.

What happens

Powerful emotions draw us into ourselves, rather than considering other people's needs or viewpoints. When we feel jealous we become preoccupied by the intensity of the feeling.

There is a paradox inherent in jealousy. We become maniacally focused on our own feelings, but at the same time, believe that the only person who can cure our jealousy is the person we are jealous of.

For example, say I have a partner who I think is very attractive. This is great, except for the fact that everywhere we go other people also find my partner very attractive. I might then find myself becoming jealous of my partner and consumed by the fear of losing them and not being sufficiently desirable enough for them. Then I get an idea that it is only by my partner telling me that I am their one and only that my jealousy will lessen. So I might badger and nag them into telling me this. However, even if this does happen, eventually a niggling question arises: 'Do I really believe what they have just told me or do I think they have just said those words to please me or get me off their back?' Jealous feelings don't give up without a fight.

The laws of jealousy

- Jealousy does not have sense of humour.
- Jealousy disregards evidence to the contrary.
- Jealousy does not like happiness or security.
- Jealousy is suspicious of your friend's intentions.
- Jealousy hates your friend's friends.
- Jealousy plays favourites and tells you that everyone is more loved than you.
- Jealousy is never satisfied or convinced.
- Friendship, love, laughter, praise and self-congratulation make jealousy sick.

- Jealousy always thinks there is a hidden agenda.
- Jealousy tries to tell you that life is a party but that you haven't been invited.
- It is a hard lesson to learn but we are the cause of our own feelings of jealousy.
- The person who is actually making me jealous is … me.

What you can do that helps

When we are jealous our self-esteem suffers. No one has ever become happy or felt worthwhile as a result of jealousy.

The source of jealousy is our own insecurity. Certainly we may have a partner who flirts but if we decide to stay in the relationship it is our insecurity that will make us jealous. Our worst and often longstanding fears haunt us. Feelings of not being enough – sexy enough, smart enough, funny enough, skinny enough, rich enough – can poison the very relationship we are trying to save.

Some of these fears and feelings of not being 'enough' have been gifted to us from childhood, such as from relatives who thought it was 'humorous' to tell a child they were a bit chunky or had sticky-out ears or were clumsy or were a bit slow to get a joke. Some of these messages echo from past relationships into current ones, creating collateral damage in the process.

Low self-esteem seeds doubt, which jealousy can help amplify and spiral out of control. Before long we might start wondering:

- Is he losing interest?
- Why is she working late?
- Why is he is so pleased when friends visit but bored when it's just the two of us?
- Why is she always so tired?

An inner voice tells us not to trust or become vulnerable to the person we feel jealous about. This is a rather wobbly concept: by remaining guarded and wary, I can't create a close and loving relationship.

For many people, jealousy runs alongside feelings of shame. All of us need to feel loved at the very times we feel least deserving. Those times are often the moments when we feel least able to ask for the love that we need. It seems shameful or belittling or unreasonable. Because of this, feelings of jealousy and envy are thrown into the shadows and we have little idea what to do with them when they arise.

To receive the real lesson of jealousy, we have to sit with the feeling. All emotions shift if you give them time. If you can, welcome them, honour them and ask them why they are here. You are not trying to manage your emotions but to let them flow through you and do their work.

Jealousy usually occurs when there is a threat to your personal security. If you can sit with the feeling long enough, you might find yourself asking questions such as:

- What lies could my feelings of jealousy be telling me?
- What truths could my feelings of jealousy be telling me?
- How does my feeling highlight an area of insecurity within myself?
- What has been betrayed?
- What needs to be restored?
- What do I need to pay attention to?
- What, if anything, do I need to do?
- What work do I need to do to feel more secure? (Not what someone else can do; what I can do.)

Jealousy is a combination of intuition and self-protection, and it is a signal to make corrective and healing actions. It can give us motivation to grow.

The jealous brain

Jealousy can cause stress and triggers the brain to release adrenaline and cortisol causing a fight-or-flight response. This is why feeling possessive of somebody can make you feel so anxious or hurt.

Jealousy also activates the brain's cingulate cortex and the lateral septum, two areas that deal with bonding and social pain. Two hormones that also play a role in the creation of jealous feelings are oxytocin and vasopressin. Oxytocin is often linked to the behaviour of kindness and caring and appears to be powerfully linked to women, who tend to react more to social groups and who is in and who is out as causes of jealousy. Vasopressin affects men more powerfully than women and is linked to protectiveness. This explains why males who are new fathers can do crazy things, but can also topple over into possessive jealousy.

Kindness

Empathic, Compassionate, Caring, Tender-hearted, Thoughtful, Considerate

Obligated, Generous-hearted, Giving, Nurturing

'You never really understand a person until you consider things from his point of view ... until you climb into his skin and walk around in it.'

– Harper Lee, *To Kill a Mockingbird*

Kindness forms a bridge that reaches from one heart to another. Kindness connects us to others. It is the source of empathy, respect and caring.

What you may notice

To be callous is to be unmoved, untouched and uncaring about the situations of others. Kindness is closeness and an entry point into the lives of others.

We all start out more tender-hearted than we can bear to show. The gentle expectant heart that hoped for goodwill and reciprocity and didn't always receive it, gradually retreated. A protective casing hardened. You learned to wait cautiously for signs of goodwill in others before showing kindness back to them.

Just because your kindness retreated behind a shield doesn't mean it isn't still there. It is so much a part of who you are, it is at your core. If we could peel back all of the layers of sediment caused by disappointment, hurt and, in some cases, much worse treatment, we would all find a tender, kind heart.

In fact, it is the tough-looking people, those who try to show that they don't give a damn, who can be the most kind-hearted of all. It is the wounded who most want to hide. They are also often the most loyal. But you've got to dig deep.

As Quentin Crisp advised: 'Neither look forward where there is doubt, nor backwards where there is regret. Look inward and ask not if there is anything outside that you want but whether there is anything inside that you have not yet unpacked.'

There are times when we all have to dig deep within ourselves to be kind, rather than be hurt or become hard. Ultimately, we are all in the care of one another. Kindness involves showing care for other people by understanding their feelings and situations. But before that, kindness is a form of vulnerability. It is a strength within that says, 'Despite all the mistreatment I've experienced, I'll be kind.'

Physical signs of kindness

- eyebrow lifting and lowering
- eye contact
- dilation of pupils
- caring acts
- sympathetic smile
- softening of facial features
- mirroring of postures or expressions.

What happens

Kindness is to identify someone else as 'of your kind,' to see what you have in common. Kindness is the courage to see the original innocence in yourself and to act from that position.

Kindness defines us as humane and human. Our mirror neurons give us the capacity to see things from other people's perspectives.

Love without kindness is an empty promise. Combining both takes us to the heart of life.

Relationships are constructed on the contribution we can make to the other, not on what advantage we can gain from the other.

Kind people are not those who lack flaws, the brave are not those who feel no fear and the generous are not those who never feel selfish.

Extraordinary people are not extraordinary because they do not possess flaws. They are extraordinary because they choose to be aware of their flaws, not be defined by them, and create a better world.

Kindness is contagious. There is a ripple effect in all of our lives: quality relationships create more quality relationships. Bringing together trust, forgiveness, integrity, hope and compassion increases our capacity to create positive changes in our world. This in turn unlocks those capacities in the people around us.

Self-kindness, when combined with altruism, builds a generosity of spirit. Increasing the level of kindness to yourself as well as other people changes the world you live in. It is a positively contagious feeling. A kind act often ripples into and reverberates into the lives of others. When this is truly present in us it has the same effect on our relationships that springtime has on daffodils. And it creates peace and harmony in the world.

What you can do that helps

Allow kindness to nest in your life, because out of it will fly all sorts of possibilities. Kindness is not just a feeling; it is a way of living. The opposite of kindness is callousness and indifference.

How to increase your kindness

1. *Adopt an imaginary friend – you*

    Kindness is an inner friendship that creates outer friendships. By adopting a generosity of spirit towards your own trials and tribulations you can allow those feelings to emanate out from yourself. As one teacher once told me, 'I know I am going to make twelve big mistakes each day so when the first one happens I think to myself, one down, only eleven to go.'

2. *Be brave – how not to act from a history of hurt*

    Kindness is the state of caring about other people's wellbeing and taking action to help make their lives better and happier. It is a social glue that allows us to connect with others and build meaningful relationships with them.

When someone does something kind for us, we like them and want to cooperate with them more. When we do something kind for someone, we earn their trust and respect, and we feel better about ourselves for being a good person.

Kindness is a reciprocal relationship. It becomes a cycle that strengthens our bond with friends, family, lovers, co-workers, and acquaintances. The more we practise kindness, the easier it is.

3. Get your intentions right

Having good intentions is the first step toward being kinder toward others and building positive relationships with them. Cultivating the right attitude is often necessary before we start acting in kinder ways.

4. See life from the other person's perspective

Imagine yourself experiencing a situation from another person's perspective. How would you feel if you were them? What thoughts would you have? How would you act if you were in their shoes? By answering these questions, we often understand why people act the way they do.

5. Practise being kind in small doses

Kindness starts as a thought but comes into being as an action. Acting kindly toward others is the most powerful way to let people know that we care about them. You don't have to be kind all of the time all of a sudden! Aim for a small act of kindness a day and build from there.

The kind brain

Kindness is hardwired into our brains.

A specific set of brain cells called mirror neurons helps us learn to replicate the behaviour we see in others. This is particularly so in kindness, where our mirror neurons not only help us to detect emotional and social cues expressed by others, but aid us to develop those same tendencies ourselves. In this way, kindness can actually be contagious!

Loneliness

Self-reliant, Independence, Solitude, Self-care, Longing, Serenity, Disconnection

Isolation, Loss, Desertion, Worthlessness, Needy, Discarded, Unwanted, Unloved

'If you are lonely when you are alone, you are in bad company.'
– Jean-Paul Sartre

The feeling of loneliness is not dependent on your situation. It can arise in a meeting, at the dining room table, at a party, in a marriage, while talking to a friend or when you are alone. It is often accompanied by a gnawing sense of loss, emptiness and lack of self-worth. It is very different to solitude, which has its own sense of time and belonging. Loneliness is a feeling of separation and disconnection.

What you may notice

We are all at risk of loneliness. The splintering of families, the dissolving of social groups and the increased focus on career and a lowered focus on friendship mean that we are all, potentially, collateral damage in the race for individual achievement.

The thought of not being wanted or needed by anyone can strike at the very heart of people. We are, by nature, social creatures, who want to be meaningfully useful to others.

Loneliness in the short-term is a personal test of our fortitude and self-reliance. We feel empty, alone and unsupported. We often shrink and feel smaller than we truly are. It is not surprising that one of the most painful of punishments has traditionally been exile, banishment and isolation. This is why enduring prolonged loneliness can be life-threatening. It is also not surprising, therefore, that some of children's greatest fears revolve around abandonment, rejection and isolation.

In the hyper-connected world, people have lost the art of being alone and content. In a society where many people are preoccupied with their phones and what's coming through their ear buds, the art of greeting others and enquiring about them seems to be eroding.

What happens

When we feel lonely, we react as if our sense of identity has been threatened. For some people, this can be terrifying and traumatising. In fact, without the distraction of screens and phones, many people describe time alone as a form of dull torture.

Our feelings have the capacity to make us contract and shrink into a smaller world or expand into a larger one. Generally people are happiest and most healthy when their sense of who they are and the world they live in is expanding.

Lonely people are more vulnerable to stress, may not relate to others well and have lower levels of synaptogenesis, the development of connective pathways, in their brains.

Physical signs of loneliness

- despair
- irregularity of eating and sleeping
- decreased immune function (especially if lonely and grieving or rejected)
- decreased dental hygiene
- risk of increased alcohol or drug use.

What you can do that helps

The sense of loneliness is the exact opposite of the feelings of connection and belonging. Belonging is the underpinning of resilience.

This means that one of the wisest investments any of us can make is in the area of relationships. When we have relationships that we feel support us, connect us and help us to belong, we are protected by a shield that helps us rise above tough times.

You could conduct an archaeological dig of your history of hurts to uncover layers of events or people who have contributed to your fears of loneliness. Alternatively, you could just accept that all of us have times when we feel overlooked, slighted, ridiculed and abandoned. We all fear loneliness to some extent.

If you feel you spend too much time fearing loneliness and abandonment, you may wish to re-secure yourself. This is a bit like installing a bigger anchor on a boat to secure it to the seabed.

The first thing to do is to spend six weeks not doing what you usually do. For example, one attempt we often use to avoid feeling abandoned is to reject others before they reject us. If you are someone who avoids closeness or sabotages anybody's attempts to get close to you, allow them to do so. Send out invitations. Even if they are rejected, you will opening yourself up to the possibility of connection.

Another way people attempt to avoid feelings of abandonment is by filling up all the space in relationships. By talking at people rather than with people, we can avoid hearing things we don't want to hear. For six weeks, be brave. Ask questions. Become a good listener. Allow silences to occur. If you have been known as a jokester who tries to lighten any moment with a good line or laugh, give yourself six weeks off from that job. You may be surprised to learn that people want to know the serious side of you, as well as the funny side.

It is often by clarifying the contribution we can make to society that we strengthen our connection to life.

If you feel the people in your life are too capricious and untrustworthy to do this with, anchor yourself to something, rather than someone. Find a community, cause, mission, interest or passion and devote yourself, as much as you can, for six weeks to it. It is often by clarifying the contribution we can make to society that we strengthen our connection to life.

The world has lost its collective ability to savour solitude. Switching off, even for a few minutes, induces a panic of 'What do I do now?'

The constant round-the-clock reliance on others for affirmations cannot be healthy. But the 24-hour world of connectivity does not actually reduce the loneliness, it only amplifies its intensity.

This can help us to understand the depths of loneliness but it doesn't lessen the intensity of the feeling. Remember: loneliness is a feeling, not a fact.

There is a great difference between being alone and being lonely. The answer to loneliness is not always surrounding yourself with other people. It is more about your relationship with yourself.

Much of the advice people are given about overcoming loneliness seems designed to turn isolated introverted people into outgoing happy-go-lucky extroverts. Some of the strategies below may work for you:

1. Getting out and going for a walk, especially in the mornings and evenings.
2. Focusing on what you have, rather than what you don't.
3. Read, join a book club or your local library.
4. Consider walking groups and movie groups.
5. Get a friendly pet you can take for a walk.
6. Get involved in your local community.

Of course we should never forget the advantages of being by yourself:

1. The only socks, clothes and dishes you need to wash are your own.
2. If someone has squeezed the toothpaste the wrong way, you know who did it.
3. When you get your bills, you aren't paying for someone else.
4. You can go out, veg out, stay out, stay in, lie in for as long as you want.
5. No one ever drinks the last of the milk without you knowing.

The biggest danger in living alone is rigidity. You can be so used to doing things in your own way that you begin to expect other people to comply. The risk is you can build a life that is so independent, there simply isn't room for anyone else.

How to be alone without being lonely

1. Develop a deeper awareness of yourself. Tune into the ebb and flow of your feelings. Particular music, movies, mementos, TV shows or

memories should be embraced while others are best left for times when you feel differently.

2. Tune into nature through gardening or being involved with animals. Nature doesn't lie; social media almost always does.
3. Concentrate on your spirituality and purpose.
4. Increase creativity. Solitude is the best time to get things done, so don't waste it.
5. Enjoy an increased sense of freedom.
6. Greet people well.
7. Say yes to invitations whenever you can.

The company we should feel most comfortable with is our own.

Loneliness and the brain

Although it is not fully understood how the neural pathway of loneliness works in the brain, it has been linked with two key brain changes: the build-up of beta-amyloid and tau proteins. As loneliness is often a cause for psychological distress, it can trigger the biological stress response, which causes the increase of these proteins. Not coincidentally, the increase of beta-amyloid and tau also appears in people who have forms of dementia. Therefore loneliness, along with repetitive negative thinking, high blood pressure, inflammation and poor sleep, are often described as possible causes of Alzheimer's or other dementia diseases.

Love

Warm-hearted, Generous, Open, Passionate, Inspirational, Intimacy, Charmed, Lust

Connected, Protected, Respected, Desire, Lustful, Obsessed, Enchanted, Attracted

One of the oldest poems we know of is about love:

> *'Oh would I were the sea wind*
> *And you upon the beach*
> *Would bare your breast to me and let me blow*
> *Until your heart I reach.'*

– FA Wright, *The Oxford Book of Greek Verse*

When love erupts into your life, it is like a new beginning. Previously, there may have been isolation, but now there is deep connection. Anxiety is often replaced with confidence and courage. Hesitancy is discarded in favour of certainty. Sadness is overcome by joy. We stand on tippy-toes full of life and anticipation. Love awakens you to a world and a place within yourself, a place that you may have forgotten even existed.

Of all of the aspects of a great life, love is the most important. All of our feelings stem from two basic states: fear (pain) and love. Strangely we are often more comfortable speaking about our pains and fears than our loves.

Having the love and commitment of a special person is life's greatest and most precious gift. It is the greatest and most precious prize that any of us can aspire to in this life. It is a prize of far greater worth and far more satisfying than any material prize or social distinction or fame or other such illusions. Love is the voice of survival. It is the song the universe sings to itself.

So guard love carefully. Protect it, care for it, allow it to grow, nurture it. Give it time and give it space.

Plato originally proposed that we were once all pairs of beings but at some point become separated. This is why we often spend our lives searching for the missing other half of ourselves.

Physical signs of love

- a tingling sense of life
- excited and full of energy
- feeling invincible
- foot wagging (couples in love often sit with their legs mirroring one another and their feet moving slightly up and down, which seems slightly similar to dogs wagging their tails when they meet another dog they like)
- dilated pupils.

What you may notice

The arrival of love rearranges your life. Whether it strikes you like a thunderbolt or creeps up slowly, it puts magic in your eyes. It focuses you and coalesces even the most scattered and distant parts of you. You feel whole.

We live in a world that is impoverished in its vocabulary. Sanskrit had at least 96 words for different forms of love, the Persians had 80. We, of course, have one. This means that all too often we practise the art of love but use a diminished vocabulary. Ancient Greek has six main words for different forms of love:

1. *Eros* or sexual passion
2. *Philia* or deep friendship
3. *Ludus* or playful love, which includes the affectionate playful banter between friends and the frivolity of dancing with other people
4. *Agape* or selfless love for everyone (*agape* was translated into the Latin word *caritas*, the base of our word 'charity')
5. *Pragma* or enduring love
6. *Philautia* or love of the self (it was recognised that this can come in two main forms: an unhealthy narcissistic obsession with yourself; or as increased capacity for wider love).

Distilling all these to one word means that we focus almost exclusively on romantic love. In doing so, we vastly reduce the importance of our love of family and children, love between friends, love of art and music, love of nature and love of meaningful pursuits. Consider how many songs are devoted to falling in or out of romantic love and how few are about other forms of love. Bruno Mars' song 'Count on Me' or 'In My Life' by the Beatles are rare exceptions. Not to mention that the glaring absence of a specific word for 'the love of chocolate' should be keeping linguists up at night.

By focusing on the external forms of desire and love we lose something very important: the ability for people to look within themselves for nourishment, energy and solace. We risk having people who are dependent and focused only on the external and not fully formed as people who value their own uniqueness.

Thinking about other people's love choices is also interesting. People's choice of partners tells you a lot about them. Some will choose a cheer squad, others a leader (or a follower), some a muse, some a younger version of themselves, and yet others a controller. Even in this we often disregard love between older people. The cynical dismissal of partnerships that occur in later life as being ones that seek a nurse, a purse or a curse, disregards the concept of mature love in our society.

What happens

Relationships can be scary. Some won't be right for you but being loving is never wrong. Love is the only safety. The true enemy is your failure to love enough.

If you are not able to become fully formed as a person and value what is unique about yourself, you not only fail to live out the life that is truly yours, you might also form relationships that place limits and barriers between you and your partner. You run the risk of settling down into a prison of the mediocre. Limits and barriers can give the illusion of security and fidelity but take you away from thriving to merely surviving.

I once heard a wonderful story that Mozart wrote a symphony so structurally perfect, so harmonically balanced, that it was actually boring. He decided to improve it by putting in some notes that were too long and others that were slightly off key, just to give the piece a liveliness and richness that he felt it lacked.

It can be the same with people. It is not that we are flawed but more that we fail to look within and develop an awareness of our interior world that creates the damage. All too often people create relationships that constrict their growth instead.

All relationships have flaws and all relationships get stuck at some point. No human can live up to the idealised projection that occurs in early love. After the wonder of finding the 'perfect' person, some of the reality of life and failings becomes apparent. This is the opportunity provided by love to grow, learn, accept and continue to love. It is also one of the many lessons of Jane Austen's famous novel *Pride and Prejudice*.

Partners, wives, husbands, boyfriends and girlfriends are rarely able to remedy flaws in one another. At best they can compensate and make do. We all need to forgive our partners for their flaws and hope like crazy that they will forgive ours. Remind yourself of how many times you have been forgiven.

I have seen some wonderful couples in therapy, sweet people, lovely people, who fell head over heels in love at school and were too polite or too damn nice to break up the relationship. Perhaps it was from fear of loneliness or fear of not finding someone else. Perhaps they were just putting the other person first and not being true to themselves. But by their thirties and forties, these couples are not developed as individuals. They have confused being close with being similar, and live in relationships that bore and stifle them.

Society's obsession with romantic love distracts people from learning how to love themselves.

Society's obsession with romantic love distracts people from learning how to love themselves. For young people this means that when their first treasured love falls apart they are devastated and alone in a way that makes them feel despair. They risk finding life not worth living or rush into the arms of another in a way to soothe the wound of their own loneliness. But that is not the answer. For people to be truly loving and compassionate to others, they first need to love and be good to themselves. They need to develop an enthusiasm for themselves.

Love belongs inside yourself and very few people realise this. It is the great message of Shakespeare's *Romeo and Juliet*: take care of yourself or lose everything. When we neglect the things that matter to us, they become the matter with us.

Love is not only blind; it has a lot of imagination. As Gabriel Garcia Marquez once said of his wife, 'I know her so well by now I have no idea who she actually is.' There is a mystery and a curiosity to love that often culminate in soft recognition. In the end love is not just about finding the right person; it is about being the right person.

Love brings with it a sense of completion. Loving yourself well will help dissolve your ego: you will no longer need to feel superior. When we love ourselves well we don't need to claim ownership of our territory: it is all our territory and can be shared. The best of love is equal and empowering.

What you can do that helps

Loving well is an ambition you should really put your heart into (so to speak!). Once you've got it, it also helps to know how to keep it.

Keeping love alive requires opening your heart

Be big-hearted. Don't give pinched compliments. Be expansive. Develop a range of friends and interests.

One of the common mistakes people can make is to take the knock-about relationships they had with their siblings and replicate them in a jokey offhand manner in their intimate friendships and relationships. Our siblings play a wonderful job in smoothing out our rougher edges and sometimes deflating our opinion of ourselves but they are not good role models for what works in loving others. In order to have some independence from one another, siblings often conceal the depth of their feelings for one another. You don't need to do this. Become genuinely appreciative of all the people you love.

Live life as an invitation

Invite people to do wonderful things with you. Invitations put the adventure back into life. Consultation is good but sweeping people off their feet is better. Most people don't really want you to ask, 'Do you want to go out for dinner?' Most would prefer you to say, 'I've found a fantastic place I think you'll love. Dress up and I'll pick you up at 7 pm.'

What stops most people doing this is the fear of rejection. What will I do if they say 'no'?

So okay, maybe they didn't want to do what you suggested. Use this information to refine your future suggestions. Without becoming a serial pest, keep inviting people to participate in a wider world of possibilities.

If you are interested in someone, let them know

One of the most common dilemmas is whether to express your interest in someone or to hold back, look pensive but intriguing and hope that the person of your desires will eventually notice you. Fortunately for us all, two mathematicians got together and developed what is known as the Gale-Shapely algorithm. I could bore you with the mathematics of this (look it up if you are interested) or just tell you that their best strategy is to go up to someone you are interested in and say, 'Hi.'

I should probably mention here that your best strategy may not actually be going up to someone and saying, 'Hi, I've done research on this and according to Gale and Shapely I need to express my deep desire to get to know you better.' That might send them running into the hills!

You are carrying some emotional baggage

On the battlefield of love you may have had many victories but it is also likely you have been scarred. There are people walking around who bear the scars of battles with you. You have hurt others and you've been hurt yourself.

Wounds of the heart can create restricted and repetitive ways of safeguarding yourself that can imperil relationships. If you are struggling to create intimate relationships, go through the process of reviewing why all the relationships you have had ended. While it may not be true in reality, for the purposes of this analysis assume that you have been the creator of that ending. Ask yourself, 'What was my role in that relationship ending?' Follow this with: 'What do I not wish to repeat?'

If you have a problem, then we have a problem

We are in the care of one another. If one person has an issue, difficulty or problem in a relationship, ideally the other person should think of it as their problem also and try and help sort it out. The world is much more complex and much more diverse than it was for our parents and grandparents and we need to be much kinder to one another.

Complete yourself

One of the great missions of human life is understanding and completing yourself. Part of this relates to respect. No one likes feeling disrespected and if you are in a relationship where you are continually treated badly you should consider leaving.

Therapists who practise Acceptance and Commitment Therapy outline that in any relationship there are four basic options:

1. Stay and change what can be changed and live by your values.
2. Stay and accept what can't be changed and live by your values.
3. Stay, give up and do things that make the relationship worse.
4. Leave the relationship and live by your values.

You need to respect yourself first before expecting it from others. Otherwise at some point you are bound to encounter resentment and bitterness. This especially applies to some of the men I see in therapy who feel disregarded by their partners. It has been described to me as the 'poor-hubby syndrome' – ie where one partner says to another, 'I need you to be home more often and I need you to earn more money.' This is a no-win paradox. In order to be home more often you will earn less; to earn more you need to be away from home. This situation requires both partners to rethink their own levels of respect and how they contribute to their relationship. Otherwise the partner who is in the no-win paradox is a bit like the cat that brings home a mouse for its owners to admire only to have the household erupt with a distinct lack of gratitude.

Choose this

It is likely that you had a choice in who was to be your partner. When times are difficult in any relationship, it's useful to remind yourself of the reasons why you chose to love this particular person. Choice is ongoing. To love well is to make that choice every day.

The loved-up brain

Three main neurotransmitters are involved in love: dopamine, oxytocin and vasopressin. When we look at the object of our love, our systems are flooded with dopamine. Oxytocin and vasopressin are more related to feelings of bonding and attachment. These are higher in the initial phase of bonding (often referred to as the honeymoon phase of romantic relationship). What is really interesting is what isn't activated in feelings of love: the amygdala, frontal cortex, parietal cortex and middle temporal cortex. The amygdala is responsible for feelings of pain, fear and anger, which might explain why we feel content in a lover's embrace. The frontal cortex is responsible for the executive functioning of judgment and logic, so if these are relaxed or not activated, we literally suspend judgment of the ones we love. This may be why the expression 'love is blind' came about!

Obsession

Rapture, Love, Devotion, Devouring, Addiction, Compulsion

Fixated, Ruminative, Compelled, Fastidious

'You become what you think about all day long.'
– Ralph Waldo Emerson

Obsessions involve unwanted or intrusive thoughts. These are thoughts that enter your head when you want to be thinking about other things and you just can't shake them off.

What you may notice

Becoming obsessed with someone or something is to give your heart totally. Obsession has a sense of rapture about it. It grips us and won't let go. It is a form of devotion. It is an enduring relationship. Obviously, not all our relationships are good for us.

Addictions preoccupy us; obsessions consume us. Gambling, train spotting, bird watching, stalking, sexual fetishes, shoes, illnesses – there is an extraordinary range of things that humans can find to obsess about. What seems quirky and odd to most people can be a source of endless fascination and total absorption to some.

Others may tire of the pursuit after a time but the obsessed person never does. They return to the object of their obsession over and over again in a pattern that Sigmund Freud called repetition compulsion.

An absorbing interest topples over into the realm of obsession when the person feels they are unable to control or stop their behaviour and that it is harmful either to themselves or to others. Interests become insistent; activities shift from optional to essential. It is compulsive. We don't control obsessions: they control us.

We can feel obsessive without suffering from obsessive compulsive disorder. For example, falling in love often causes obsessive thinking. Similarly, most of us have lain awake in bed at night thinking something over and over again that just won't let us settle down and go to sleep.

There are also cultural variations to this: what seems peculiar in one culture may be perfectly mainstream in another. For example, some cultures are more focused on the body than others. As a result they may be more health conscious but may also be more hypochondriacal than others. Indigenous Australian and New Zealand Māori cultures are much more focused on family lineage and ancestry than Caucasian cultures. The modern fascination with taking selfies would bemuse, if not perplex, even our most recent ancestors.

There are also occupational variations. What might appear as obsessional checking for most of us could be regarded as highly desirable in airline pilots and surgeons.

There are, however, some things that people, wherever they live, seem to be more likely to obsess about:

- weight loss
- exercise
- relationships
- gambling
- cleanliness
- germs and contamination
- causing harm to others
- mortality
- computer games
- sport
- sex
- physical conditions
- religious ideals.

What happens

Most of us have minds filled with chattering thoughts that flit from topic to topic. People with obsessions have a relentless grinding of the same thoughts with intense regularity. You might think this is just thinking on endless repeat but it also has a vice-like grip on the obsessed person's emotions.

Our brains are designed to form patterns, which are influenced by our feelings. The intensity of obsession occurs often because the person, activity or object of obsession becomes associated with pleasure in some form or another. That feeling of pleasure creates a 'reward' signal to our brains and we feel an urge to repeat it. The more this happens, the stronger the urge becomes, eventually turning into a compulsion.

Compulsions are actions that people take usually in order to gain some relief from their obsessive thinking. These can include hand washing, hoarding, doubting, touching surfaces in sequences, or endlessly repeating numbers or words in their minds.

What you can do that helps

When an obsession has you in its grip it will stay with you all the hours of each day. This is beautifully portrayed in Robert Louis Stephenson's *Dr Jekyll and Mr Hyde*, where gentle Dr Jekyll creates a potion that transforms him into Mr Hyde, a man without a conscience. At first delighted in his transformation, Dr Jekyll then finds himself doing things he wouldn't normally do. No matter how hard he tries, he has become involuntarily trapped in Mr Hyde's character. It is a great metaphor of how obsessions work.

Obsessions rule your awareness with maniacal power. They will chase you like the hounds of hell. The question is whether, like Mr Hyde, they will also dictate your actions.

Some obsessions could land you in prison for a long time so to resist and restrain yourself requires an enormous battle of wills. Creating firm boundaries around obsessions at least frees up some part of your life to be under your own control. This is hard work. For people who have destructive obsessions, resisting their demands is like wrestling with inner demons.

Some obsessions can be helpful

When possible, directing your obsessions into interests, collections and hobbies can be valuable. Given your compulsive tendencies you may wish to limit the amount of time you can spend on these activities.

Mix it up

Obsessions are usually singular in focus. You may be able to lessen their intensity by having several different projects on the go at once. Alternatively, broadening your interests or your repertoire of activities may help.

The obsessive brain

Obsessions are a disturbance of information processing in the brain. For most of us, a thought has a use-by date, after which we get bored and move on to another thought.

In obsessive thinking, we see what is often described as loopy thinking, where an idea sticks, rather than dissolves.

Imaging studies of people with OCD suggest that their brains function differently to those people who have other anxiety disorders or no OCD. People with OCD often have different patterns of connections in their corpus callosum (the link between the left and right hemispheres of the brain) and the cingulum (connections between different parts of the limbic system). There also seems to be a greater amount of actual grey matter between the different sections.

Another factor in loopy thinking or even OCD is the limited production of serotonin (the feel-good neurotransmitter) receptors and an increased sensitivity to the stress hormones, cortisol and norepinephrine receptors.

Pity

Caring, Compassionate, Empathy, Kindness, Commiseration

Denigrating, Sorrow, Tenderness, Mercy, Understanding, Humanity

'Life is largely grief and labour
Two things help you through:
Chortling when it hits your neighbour,
Whingeing when it's you.'

– Kingsley Amis

The word pity comes from the old French word *pite* and the Latin word *pietas*, both meaning duty. As members of communities we have a role in caring for one another.

What you may notice

Pity is a way of tuning yourself into the difficulties of others. It is a sharing in the sorrows of someone else and understanding their plight or situation. To commiserate with difficult times and misfortune is a form of caring.

If kindness is being attentive to other people, pity is being attuned to their circumstances. However, this is a complex feeling with mixed intentions. It is often a distancing feeling. It can set us apart from the people we pity. At its best it brings forth kindness and care; at its worst it brings smugness and superiority.

The dangerous sequence of pity can be:

- I pity you. I really do.
- I pity you from the bottom of my heart.
- I pity you from on high; I pity your pathetic plight.
- I despise you.

The scorn that can hide behind some forms of pity can be used to justify all manner of interventions on behalf of someone else. For example, people might say, 'We are doing this for your own good.' Often these (usually) well-intentioned interventions are neither wanted nor helpful.

Many minority groups have learned to be wary of offers of assistance that stem from pity. Pity can trap people into thinking that they know what is best for others who are suffering.

Directing the pity towards yourself and throwing your own pity-party is disastrous. Self-pity is often regarded by others as pathetic. There is a special harshness many people reserve for those who feel sorry for themselves. Despite this, it is difficult to be kind to others but not to yourself. It seems unreasonable to expect people to see the difficulties faced by others and not at the same time see some of the obstacles faced by themselves. The world is best served when people can be kind to themselves and others.

What happens

The attunement between people that allows great relationships to flourish is an antidote to the trials of the world. When you watch close friends catch up with one another, they usually check in with one another's wellbeing. Successes are celebrated, setbacks and sorrows are shared. One may pity the other. They both may pity each other. Often this pre-empts a conspiring about how to improve matters. Pity only really becomes helpful when it leads to action.

To just pity alone can disempower and disable. Confirming the victim status of the other person by offering them pity is not always helpful.

As we discussed in the section on Kindness, just co-suffering is not helpful; it is what we do with that feeling that counts.

What you can do that helps

If you are the person offering pity to someone else, move your pity into action. Roll up your sleeves and get to work doing what you can do to help that person.

If you are the person experiencing self-pity, stop telling people about it and start improving your life. Take some time to reflect and then complete the Annual Wellbeing Plan outlined in the next section on Regret.

Regret

Reflective, Saudade, Disappointed, Rueful, Saddened, Remorseful, Guilty

Nostalgia, Melancholy, Recrimination, Wistfulness, Forlorn, Anger, Loss

'Make it a rule of life never to regret and never to look back.
Regret is an appalling waste of energy; you can't build on it;
it's only good for wallowing in.'

– Katherine Mansfield

Regret is an invitation to undertake a full appreciation of the present. It is a signal to renew and restart. It is also a valuing of the opportunities of life and a reminder that time is one of our most important possessions.

What you may notice

We all learn too late. We have all wasted time, worn out good relationships, squandered resources, misspent energies, been too preoccupied by things that didn't really matter and probably invested in some people who weren't worth the time. We have all taken some of the love we have given for granted.

If only we could have been wiser at a younger age. Gordon Livingston has a great phrase (and a wonderful book) for this: 'Too soon old, too late smart'.

There is a lovely Portuguese word *saudade* that refers to a desire for something that does not and probably cannot exist, for something other than what is happening. It is a reminder that time is passing and opportunities may have been missed.

Short-term regrets are usually about things we did that ended badly. Long-term regrets are more often based on things that we didn't do. Regret is a strange emotion in that, unlike anger, sadness or happiness, it only happens in hindsight or after an event. Regret is a by-product of reflection, and as such has no real influence over a particular event as it is happening. It does serve a purpose by signalling what you might want to change in the future, what to prepare for and what you don't want to happen again. However, if you dwell too long on a regret you run the risk of getting stuck and losing forward momentum. As well-known US children's author Libba Bray says: 'We all do things we desperately wish we could undo. Trying to change the past is like chasing clouds and, like chasing clouds, dwelling on regret can use up a lot of our emotional bandwidth without really anything to show for it.'

What happens

There is a famous cartoon of two dogs in front of a kennel. One says to the other, 'Wow, you had a bad nightmare last night.' The other dog shudders and replies, 'Yes it was awful. I dreamt I was a human.'

Being human is no bed of roses. Many of the things people want most in life are in conflict with each other. We want to eat chocolate but also be thin. We want to travel the world and have adventures but save our money to become wealthy. We want to feel secure but also be free. We want money but not have to work for it. We want to be in close, caring communities but not have nosy neighbours. This makes it a bit tricky to get through life without experiencing a few regrets.

Regrets can come quickly or slowly. Sending a furious email can be the cause of instant regret. Never telling someone important that you love them can smoulder inside you for a lifetime.

What you can do that helps

Kicking yourself in the backside for having regrets is like blaming yourself for being human.

In some parts of Africa there is a ritual around regrets. At the end of the year, you dig a hole in the ground and you tell it all your regrets:

- 'I didn't get to buy the sports car.'
- 'I didn't get a promotion.'
- 'I didn't lose weight.'
- I didn't ask that person out.'

Once you have spoken all of your regrets into the hole you fill it up with soil and plant a flowering bush so that something beautiful can emerge.

Another possibly more practical and helpful way to deal with regrets is to take a piece of paper and create two columns. In the left column list all of your regrets. Then title the right column, Lessons. Write down the lessons you can draw from the regrets and use them to shape your future.

Regret can also stir you into action to make meaningful plans so you don't miss out on the important priorities in life. One way is to create a plan for maximising your life, as outlined on the next page.

Annual wellbeing plan

This is designed to help you establish clear plans and priorities to increase your personal wellbeing over the next year.

Looking after yourself

Please rate how well you are currently looking after yourself:

0   10

Really well   Really badly

Now indicate what number you would like to achieve by the end of the year:

Please write down something you could do to increase this area of your wellbeing in each of the following areas.

Something I will do more of:	Something I will do less of:	Something I will start doing:	Something I will stop doing:

Important connections

Please rate how well you are currently connected to the people who are important to you.

0	10
Really well	Really badly

Now indicate what number you would like to achieve by the end of the year:

Please write down something you could do to increase this area of your wellbeing in each of the following areas.

Something I will do more of:	Something I will do less of:	Something I will start doing:	Something I will stop doing:

Do the same exercise for the following areas in your life: Calmness, Focus, Looking after your body and Energy levels. Now you need to implement these ideas to make a difference to your wellbeing. Ideally, you will review your progress at least once a month.

Rejection

Dejection, Disappointment, Banishment, Invisibility, Abandonment

Fragmented, Self-focused, Hurt, Scared, Timid

'Was I bitter? Absolutely. Hurt? You bet your sweet ass I was hurt. Who doesn't feel a part of their heart break at rejection. You ask yourself every question you can think of, what, why, how come, and then your sadness turns to anger. That's my favourite part. It drives me, feeds me, and makes one hell of a story.'

–Jennifer Salaiz

Rejection is often described as the act of pushing someone or something away. There are many forms of rejection, including romantic rejection, social rejection and rejection from one's family. It can occur on a large or small scale in everyday life. While it is viewed as a part of life, some people deal with it more easily than others.

What you may notice

Some people live their entire lives trying not to be rejected. In the process they resemble human chameleons, shifting their persona or social masks to resemble any group they are with. They will laugh at jokes they don't find funny and appear to endorse ideas and opinions they secretly can't abide. Their concealment renders their real selves invisible. But where would this sort of behaviour stem from? An early harsh experience of rejection has left them so hurt and wounded they will sacrifice everything, including the truth of themselves, to avoid being rejected again.

Some of our social chameleons have grown up in families where every one of their needs has been reinterpreted for them. A controlling family member said something like, 'You don't really need a drink; you actually need an ice-cream.' When this interaction occurs repeatedly, a child learns that there is no point having an independent view or opinion and eventually questions the validity of their own wishes.

Modifying your position to fit in sells you short. You become fragmented and eventually have little idea of who you are or what you stand for. Instead, you become a great reader of people in order to anticipate their points of view and find ways to agree with them. This is the art of a master marketing guru – maximum acceptability, minimal authenticity and zero chance of rejection. If this sounds at all familiar, you might like to read the section on Identity and Belonging on page 149.

Living your life as a reaction, rather than your own unique creation, hollows you out. It is like putting up a sign in your inner world reading 'Space to occupy'.

Living your life as a reaction, rather than your own unique creation, hollows you out.

You might think a life like this would be calm and agreeable. Just fit in and agree with everyone. Instead, it often becomes confused and volatile. Firstly, people often come in groups and they may not agree on everything. Then you have the anxiety of who to please and fit in with most. Secondly, very few of us are great at total sacrifice to others. Eventually the mighty 'I' recoils from all this obsequiousness and servitude and lashes out. These episodes are then often viewed with guilt and self-loathing.

Even more troubling is that when you are willing to do anything to avoid rejection, the worst types of people pick up on it and target you.

What happens

Of course we will be rejected. Everyone has been. There are jobs we are not going to get, romances that won't work out, teams we won't be selected for, invitations that won't be issued, and good friends who turn out to be not so good after all. Life has a nasty way of making you learn how to cope with feelings of rejection. We can blame and denigrate people who reject us. We soon learn this doesn't help.

Fearing rejection links to the deep empty wasteland of abandonment. When we feel abandoned, we cannot love. Instead we cling in desperation to anyone or anything that offers salvation from the empty space within ourselves. This makes us vulnerable. Abusive people pick up on signs like these. Alternately offering devotion then threatening to never see us again, these people become addictive. We can't love them, but can't easily leave them.

When we define ourselves almost entirely by the opinions or judgments of others, who are we if those relationships fall apart? Who are we when those relationships become unhealthy?

The fear of rejection and abandonment is also a rejection of a part of ourselves. We can no longer access our individuality and our strength. There is a part of you that can't be defined by the acceptance of others. This requires an expanded sense of self-knowledge to find an identity that is not attributed to or defined by other people.

We all rely on our quality relationships to keep us healthy. Ideally the nature of these relationships evolves from dependence to cooperation and collaboration.

What you can do that helps

Part of life's success recipe is identifying the people who value the attributes you have and spending more time with them. It is also about identifying the people who do not value what you have to offer or who you are and spending a lot less time on them.

Not everyone is going to like you or think you could amount to much. Get used to it. Accept that it is so and then get out of their way.

Finding your own voice in a world that can't listen

There is a freedom in saying enough is enough. It is time to reclaim the territory that is rightfully yours and the soul that is yours to inhabit fully. The time for discussion or harsh admonishments has passed. It serves no purpose now. The time for regret is over. The past needs to make way to clear a path towards a new future. The direction to take is sure but the steps are not. But you take them anyway. Occupying the only life that is yours to live. Occupying the only love that is yours to give.

Resentment

Self-pity, Brooding, Grievances, Bitterness, Rejection, Humiliation, Jealousy, Annoyance

Shame, Rage, Vengeance, Acknowledgement, Remorse, Blame, Malice, Chagrin

'It's no good crying over spilt milk;
all we can do is bail up another cow.'

– Ben Chifley, Australian prime minister, 1945–1949

Resentment is a very strong feeling. It can stem from a range of situations but the common denominator is that it involves a sense of injustice and/ or being hard done by. It is often associated with feelings of anger, rage, sadness or bitterness.

What you may notice

Resentment is always about comparison. Your talents and attributes haven't been recognised or appreciated and you feel overlooked and hard done by. The imaginary scales of life have been tipped against you. It is the sense that someone, somewhere, is getting more than their fair share and it isn't you. A common cry seems to be, 'It's all right for them but what about me? I deserve better.'

Keeping a tally of life is always a bad idea. No matter how objective we think we are as accountants of life's tally sheet, we tip the scales against ourselves. We are more attuned to the times when things didn't go as we wished than the times that went well. Slights, missed opportunities, feelings of rejection and times when things just didn't work out can leave us wallowing in a cesspit of our own self-pity.

People are highly vulnerable to resenting their siblings. This can play out in terms of who is the favourite or who is loved more. This is why unequal inheritances usually split families.

People don't like to show that they are feeling resentful. It is much easier to view yourself in the more favourable light of being the aggrieved victim of a terrible injustice.

Resentment holds people in a passive state of avoidance and also keeps their focus on the past. If you truly feel injustices are being done, start a social campaign to change things. Don't sit at home brooding over unfairness, perceived or otherwise.

The by-products of resentment are many: desire for revenge, punishment, vengefulness, outrage, fury, wrath, hostility, ferocity, bitterness, alienation, hate, loathing, scorn and spite.

Physical signs of resentment

As resentment is often a hidden feeling, there are no clear facial or physical signs. Some rough indicators include:

- eyes narrowed
- sour expression
- tight feeling in chest and stomach
- headaches and stomach-aches
- sleep disturbances
- pessimistic outlook.

What happens

Resentment can be more than a feeling; it can become a way of life. It is the begrudging pursuit of inferiority. Others always appear luckier, prettier, smarter, shrewder, and have happier lives. Worse still, they had it much easier than you! Rather than creating a life that is fulfilling, it is easier to stop trying and start resenting.

With resentment, you are always living in the past. The problem with that, of course, is that you can't change the past.

The French word *ressentir* describes the act of feeling again. The grievances that have occurred seem to flare up in vivid and compelling ways. It doesn't take much rekindling of the feeling to experience the full force of your resentment.

All of us, if we were being particularly self-sabotaging, could summon up a list of times when things went against us: the time when I didn't get selected for the team, wasn't voted for, or didn't get the top marks, the jobs I wasn't asked to do, the promotions I didn't get, the sacrifices I had to make, the people who didn't want to go out on a date with me … The list is potentially endless. We might adopt a role of being a vengeful angel where we try to redress inequities that have been dealt to us. We could find other people who also feel overlooked and form a type of aggrieved vigilante group.

> **All of us, if we were being particularly self-sabotaging, could summon up a list of times when things went against us.**

Shakespeare's *King Lear* is a tale of the personal tragedy of resentment. Lear asked his three daughters how much they loved him, only to end up resenting the reply of his youngest and favourite daughter, Ophelia. He banishes her from his kingdom, which then leads him to abandon his throne and wander aimlessly through the desert slowly going mad with resentment. Similarly, the final stages of the first Trump presidency seem to have involved a frustrated mob being incited to violence by a resentful and unaccepting leader.

In a personal sense, resentment often leads to an unhappy inactivity where nothing seems fair and there is an emphasis on collecting more and more evidence to prove ourselves right.

For societies, the politics of resentment are dangerous. When economic inequality and wage uncertainty rise, there is always a risk that society will fragment into groups, with some groups feeling that they are missing out or being overlooked by others who are benefitting. This usually divides societies along the lines of us (people in the same position as ourselves) and them (people in dissimilar positions).

This doesn't mean citizens shouldn't aspire to create a fairer society for all. However, when resentment predominates, passivity and blame creep in. Us-and-them thinking divides people. Us-and-them thinking is the basis of sexism, racism and domestic violence.

To maintain resentment, you need to have someone to resent. Those who bear the brunt of resentment most, are often those who deserve it least, such as homeless people, drug addicts, refugees and disabled people.

What you can do that helps

Become an activist rather than a pessimist. Don't wait for someone else to improve your world. Look for ways you can actively change the things in your life that you are unhappy with. One of the sure-fire ways to become resentful is to wait for an inheritance to improve your life. It will stunt your life, as you may hold off on doing anything to improve yourself or your situation and miss out on developing emotional independence and resilience.

Think long and hard about the question, 'Does the world owe me anything?'

By hanging on to resentment, you run the risk of settling into avoidant mode and miss out on some of the great opportunities of your life.

Even if you never admit to it publicly, honestly confessing your resentment to yourself is helpful. It will clear the space in your soul to start focusing on becoming the change you want to see.

Consider what you have and write down the things in your life you appreciate and feel grateful for. Practise acknowledging these as often as you can.

Time to move on

If resentment is fixed and unshifting, the best thing you may be able to do is to mentally move beyond it and channel your energies into something else. As Frank Sinatra once said, 'The best revenge is massive success.'

Sadness

Sombre, Helpless, Despair, Sorrow, Anguish, Gloomy, Glum, Suffering, Despondent

Discouraged, Morose, Resigned, Hopelessness, Miserable, Forlorn

My sorrow, when she's here with me
Thinks these dark days of autumn rain
Are beautiful as days can be.
She loves the bare, the withered tree;
She walks the sodden pasture lane.

– Robert Frost, *My November Guest*

Sadness is characterised by feelings of unhappiness and a lowered mood. It is a natural response to any situation that is painful, upsetting or disappointing. Sadness can be intense or mild, depending on the circumstances. It is usually temporary.

What you may notice

Happiness is apparently something that requires pursuing, whereas feelings of melancholy and sadness creep up on us. It takes courage to turn in towards our own sadness, but the lessons it can teach us are profound. Knowing not to be scared of sadness but to acknowledge its presence and its reality allows us to live a full life.

We are more focused when we feel sad. Our senses sharpen and we have a heightened sensitivity. It is like Rembrandt's painting technique of adding darker shadows to create contrasting lightness. While we may not feel it at the time, periods of sadness give us rest and prepare us for the next sense of possibility.

Sadness calls to us and we seek it out. Many forms of music, especially the blues, mimic the human voice in despair. Sadness is something we all have at times. It connects people in powerful ways. It is a common human experience.

Sadness is a yearning, a connecting with poignancy and loss. It is a time of subdued reflection and consideration. It can be morose but can also be bitter-sweet. It can be a time when you cherish what has been and feel sad for its passing but are also acutely aware of its value. There are moments when we can almost enjoy the acute sensitivity that sadness gives us.

Using the term depression to describe feeling sadness is dangerous. They are not the same feeling.

We attune ourselves to the transience of all things and often give more attention to endings rather than beginnings. If we allow sadness too much indulgence, it can ruin our enjoyment, but in select doses it makes us acutely aware that things are precious and don't last forever. As Dylan Thomas put it, 'The tree is felled in the acorn.'

An old proverb says that we can't prevent the birds of sadness from flying over our heads but we can prevent them making nests in our hair.

We often rush past sadness, amplify it and describe ourselves as being depressed. Using the term depression to describe feeling sadness is dangerous. They are not the same feeling. In fact, they have little to do with one another. We all have times of sadness. A much smaller percentage of people become depressed.

Sadness, if you can bear to sit with it for a while, has lessons to teach us. It arises at times of uncertainty when we need to change something about ourselves or the way we do things. In contrast, depression is a disabling, disconnecting affront to our senses. Sleep, energy, appetite, sociability and desire are all victimised by depression. Depressed people experience changes in metabolism, higher levels of glucocorticoids, disorganised sleep patterns and loss of functioning.

Women, children who have lost a parent, chronic pain sufferers and people with ambivalent grief (as in 'I miss them but now I can get on with my life') are at high risk of depression. The great paradox about depression is that you become preoccupied with yourself and at the same time you don't care about yourself. You become preoccupied by the very thing you don't care about.

Depression is not just a happiness deficiency. If you could add happiness to a depressed person they wouldn't be able to hold on to it. Depression is woundedness and often a response to being deeply hurt or treated badly.

Physical signs of sadness

- tired, lethargic
- loss of pleasure
- empty
- crying
- shuddering
- difficulty swallowing

- breathlessness
- sighing
- droopy eyelids
- lips turned downwards
- eyebrows contracting
- down-turned mouth.

What happens

For all of us, our emotions have ups and downs. Some people, though, are more prone to patterns of happiness followed by sadness, which could be due to what is known as psychological inflation and deflation. Inflation is a time of feeling pumped up with a sense of being more powerful than perhaps you really are. Deflation is like the air escaping a balloon: you feel lessened, diminished and sometimes desolate.

No amount of accolades, possessions or positive thinking will protect you from sadness. The Greek myth of King Midas is a great example of inflation and deflation. When the king was granted a wish that everything he touched turned to gold, he was beyond happy. He believed he would become the richest man in the world! However, you can't eat food made of gold, smell the scent of a flower made out of gold or receive love from a statue. He was plunged into the depths of despair and died of starvation. The very thing that made him happy also made him sad and, eventually, dead.

People who are prone to the inflation–deflation rollercoaster of emotions usually need to work with someone to help them step around their own ego and find a way to contribute to life more meaningfully. Otherwise, self-admiration almost invariably leads to self-denigration.

What you can do that helps

There was a contest of wisdom once held in Ancient Greece to find someone who could write down a sentence that would always be true. The winning sentence was 'This too will pass.'

There are times of sadness in everyone's life. It is curious that people who come to me for therapy afflicted by sadness usually want the sadness to end, but vigorously defend their pursuit of the very things that are making them sad. Perhaps they are following an inner wisdom that says some sad times are necessary. Sadness can be a creative rather than a destructive feeling. Many great works of art, music and poetry had their roots in melancholic times.

Sadness is a time to take stock. It is not about being cheered up, told to get over it or joked out of it. Absorb the sadness. Try not to become consumed or overwhelmed by it. It will pass. By sitting with your feeling of sadness and learning from it, you can deepen your understanding of yourself.

The sad brain

When the neurotransmitters serotonin and dopamine become depleted, it results in feelings of decreased happiness and lower motivation to do anything.

The limbic system (responsible for our emotional and behavioural regulation) becomes more active and the frontal lobes (responsible for planning and anticipation) become less active.

The levels of gamma-amino butyric acid (GABA) levels lower, which increases the likelihood of ruminative worrying. To top it all off, our sex hormones also decrease!

Shame

Contrite, Justice-seeking, Caring, Compassion, Culpable, Humiliation

Embarrassed, Remorseful, Mortified, Stricken, Contrite

'Shame is a soul-eating emotion.'
– Carl Jung

A feeling of shame is a clear signal that our personal equilibrium has been interrupted. Shame can induce feelings of inadequacy, regret, dishonour and unworthiness. It can be triggered by another person or by our own failings to meet a personal standard. It can motivate us to withdraw or hide ourselves away. Shame is a very unpleasant feeling and many of us try to avoid it all costs.

What you may notice

We have all felt shamed and, most likely, we have all shamed other people. Most of us learn about shame by being shamed ourselves. We then see it as a feeling that is imposed on us from the outside world.

Shame is a personal wounding that we find incredibly hard to talk about. People can feel so ashamed of being shamed they never talk about it to anyone.

There are two forms of shame:

1.   The sense of being judged by others negatively

This can cause us to be anxious, hesitant and self-conscious. It can also cause us to accept other people's standards of what is right and wrong, rather than developing our own moral compass. Some common expressions people use that have elements of shame embedded in them include: 'Tough guys don't cry', 'Nice girls don't', 'It's mean to upset people', or 'We don't get angry in this family.'

Feeling on the precipice of being evaluated negatively by someone can leave us edgy, fearful of making mistakes and perfectionistic in nature.

2. *The sense that we are not living up to our own standards*

Many of the shamed people I have worked with in my therapy room have felt haunted by something they have done in their past involving their own integrity or standards slipping. This can lead to feelings of unworthiness and inadequacy.

Of course, shame has some benefits. Many of our most important relationships have been saved by our inner warning bell of shame. Consciously being aware of shame can help us to right wrongs or set us on a course towards justice.

There is also shame that belongs to you and shame that was forced on you by others. While no emotion is without some message and use, shame is best when it is fleeting and alters our actions; when we use it to be constructive and to right wrongs. It is when it is prolonged and is linked to our sense of who we are that it becomes a problem.

Physical signs of shame

- pain in the pit of the stomach
- sense of dread
- looking down, head lowered
- wanting to shrink away or disappear
- hiding or covering part of face
- flushed skin (blushing).

What happens

Shamed people usually feel extremely self-conscious. They avert their eyes and lower their heads. New information is blocked. There is intense discomfort and muscular tension. Awareness collapses inward to protect the self and there is a shrinking of body energy. Skin may become flushed with embarrassment. There are feelings of inadequacy and the fear of self-exposure. The person wants to shrink or hide away and feels mortified. These feelings are so excruciating that people want to avoid them at all costs.

How guilt and shame are different

Guilt involves feeling bad about what you've thought or done. Shame is feeling bad about who you are.

Broadly speaking, we have cultures that base their negative interactions between people predominantly on shame and others mainly on guilt. In shame cultures, what matters is what other people think of you and people fear embarrassment and loss of face. In guilt cultures, people are more likely to fear their inner critic, the harsh inner voice of moral judgment. In shame cultures we're playing our part on the public stage. In guilt cultures we're engaged in an inner conversation with the better angels of our nature.

Shame doesn't just hurt; it damages. Ultimately shamed people become their own tormentors, constantly thinking things like: 'I'm wrong/bad/worthless/hopeless/unlovable/ugly/stupid.'

People who engage in sexual activities at a young age or who were abused sexually may develop a sense of shame about their role in these acts. Sexual abuse of children typically causes the child to feel dirty and bad. Sometimes they can even internalise the shame of the adult who committed the offence.

People often use other emotions to hide their shame and maintain self-esteem. Anger, depression, exaggerated pride, anxiety and helplessness are substituted to avoid feeling the total blackness of being bad/wrong/hopeless. Some of the angriest people are doing a frantic cover-up job on their shame.

What you can do that helps

The person who is truly shamed has no peace. They have no place to feel safe or be authentic. If you see yourself as inadequate, you spend your life trying to conceal that flaw.

Shame can rob you of a sense of belonging. You feel isolated, tainted or singularly inadequate and that separates you from people.

The power of shame is so strong that most people don't process it at all. We don't like the feeling so we stay as far away from it as possible. Sadly, life has an uncanny knack of making sure that we end up having to confront the very things we try to run away from.

Shame never makes anyone feel better; it only induces more shame. What if you feel you have done something that is truly shameful?

- Work it through with a therapist you can trust.
- Keep a record or confession somewhere.
- Conduct a conversation between the part of you that feels shamed and the part of you that does not (see the section on Acceptance).
- Use your past acts as a catalyst to do good in the world.
- Act to restore your dignity and, where possible, repair the damage you may have caused.

Whether you have been the unlucky recipient of a life event that has caused you to feel shame, or you feel shame as a consequence of your own actions, below are some steps to help you visualise how your shame is working and how to overcome it.

The eclipse model of working with shame

Most of us have problems because life presents us with an endless stream of them: dentists to be seen, work to go to, washing to be done and so on.

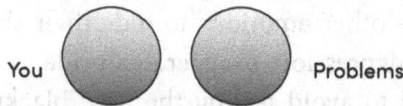

You   Problems

People who feel shame have an overlap between themselves and the problem. They no longer are people who have a problem, they *are* the problem.

You   Problems

Shame can loom so powerfully over all your other emotions, you no longer really see who you are; you only see the shame. You are eclipsed by the problems.

You ⬤⬤ Problems

Initially, reconnecting with all the things that are good in you starts to de-eclipse this relationship. If you can't do this emotionally, you can take physical action by doing things that remedy the shameful behaviour. For example, if you have stolen money from a charity, you might start anonymously donating time and money to a similar charity.

You ⬤⬤ Problems

By doing things that enable you to respect yourself more, you further de-eclipse the shame. You are more than the shameful act.

When we talk about shameful things, they lose their power. Bring the shame to a conscious level by recognising where it is located in the body.

Describe to someone the original experience that caused the shame. Try to feel all the feelings associated with your shame. Describe the hurt, sadness, revenge and embarrassment. Your shame might have outnumbered everything else to the point where it is hard to identify what you actually feel other than shame. Be conscious of this and know that it might take some time. Shame works hard to keep everything covered.

You ⬤⬤ Problems

If you keep doing this, eventually you will unlink yourself almost totally from the shame. You will need to keep protecting the emerging sense of who you are, as shame stops people from developing.

You   Problems

And then usually something interesting happens! For many people, familiarity is more important than growth, so just when you are almost totally free of the shame, you might find yourself in the position to do something shameful again.

If you are not careful, you could easily go back to being eclipsed by shame. Again, it pays to be aware of this possibility.

You   Problems

The last part of freeing yourself from the history of shame is to begin respecting who you are and have others respect what you stand for. Moving through the process of differentiating yourself from your shame will help you begin to respect yourself. Once others sense you have self-respect they will respect you accordingly.

Shame and the brain

When we are shamed it affects the activation levels of our insular cortex. As mentioned earlier, this part of the brain is involved in the feeling of disgust. Sadly, this explains why some people who were abused or shamed as children develop mental health issues relating to self-loathing, self-harm, addiction, chronic fatigue, fibromyalgia, body image issues, irritable bowel syndrome and anxiety.

When we are deeply shamed our dorsal vagal complex becomes activated. This the part of our stress response system that shuts us down and immobilises us when we are terrified. Some shamed people have times when they simply can't move or do anything. Others have times of dissociation when they feel extremely disconnected from their identity and feelings. This is why asking, 'Why didn't they do something?' about someone who has been sexually assaulted is not only insulting; it also shows a lack of understanding about human biology.

Surprise

Contrite, Justice-seeking, Caring, Compassion, Culpable, Humiliation

Embarrassed, Remorseful, Mortified, Stricken, Contrite

'Searching is half the fun: life is much more manageable when thought of as a scavenger hunt as opposed to a surprise party.'

– Jimmy Buffett

Surprise is a strong alert signal that tells us that there is something important about this moment and we have to pay attention.

What you may notice

Few feelings divide people as much as surprise. Some people love surprises; others hate them. Imagine for a moment that you were called up on stage by a rock star. Would you be filled with fear or delighted?

Most us are drawn to being surprised – it's just the amount that varies. Some people love the thrill of a horror movie, while others are behind the couch with their eyes covered. Others still like their surprises packaged in safe ways. For example, they may enjoy a murder mystery as long as the plot, the setting and the characters give them a reassuring sense that all will end well.

Well-known English crime writer Agatha Christie was the mistress of surprise. Her murder mystery stories often placed grisly murders in lovely familiar settings. Ironically, Agatha Christie herself was the cause of much surprise when she went missing for 11 days. After a massive investigation and worldwide newspaper coverage, she was discovered some four hours' drive away in Harrowgate, living under an assumed identity with no apparent recall of who she was. She never spoke about what happened to her during those 11 days, leaving a mystery that even one of her famous fictional detectives could not have solved.

There are two main kinds of surprise:

1. Perceptual mismatch between what we see and our expectations of what we thought we would see.
2. Astonishment at unexpected events, generated when an event is in contrast with the previous long-term knowledge and expectation.

Physical signs of surprise

- shock
- laughing
- shrieking or screaming
- anger
- fear
- jumping
- shaking
- trembling
- loss of balance
- blurred vision
- nausea.

What happens

Surprise begins with a shock that can be almost fearful, and is usually accompanied by a surge of adrenaline. Some people are able to quickly re-interpret the event and receive a rush of dopamine, causing a pleasurable response. For others, the sensation of being unsettled and threatened remains.

Being surprised causes humans to physically freeze for 1/25th of a second.

When we're surprised, our emotions intensify. If we're surprised by something positive, we'll feel more intense feelings of happiness or joy. If we're surprised by something negative, our feelings of anger, despair or unhappiness will also be heightened.

Surprise is sensitivity turned outwards. It demands attention. Surprise hijacks all of our mental processes and pulls our focus into one thing. Surprise can help us learn by facilitating curiosity. Surprise also builds new neural pathways in our brains, leading us to think more flexibly and creatively.

Surprise feeds our novelty bias. Mostly we like new, shiny, interesting things and will seek them out. This is partly why scanning social media posts can be so compelling. We are not that different from a bird who is transfixed by a mirror tied to a branch, moving in the breeze.

When we invite surprise into our lives on a regular basis, we elevate our mood.

What you can do that helps

A recent study from the University of California, Berkeley, found that those people who experience more awe in their life – a type of surprise experienced when we find something impressive or powerful – may be healthier. Specifically, the researchers found that the 'awe' group had lower levels of interleukin–6 (IL–6), a chemical that promotes inflammation, in their bodies.

If you are interested in breaking out of old patterns and discovering new experiences that will surprise you about yourself in positive ways, there are two great books I recommend. The first is Nick Bantok's *The Trickster's Hat: A Mischievous Apprenticeship in Creativity*. The second is the more well-known but wonderful Julia Cameron's *The Artist's Way*.

Suspicion

Cautious, Considered, Watchful, Guarded, Angry, Doubtful

Jealous, Wary, Combative, Competitive, Self-protective, Defensive

'My body has certainly wondered a good deal,
but I have an uneasy suspicion that my mind has not
wondered enough.'

– Noel Coward

Suspicion is an indicator of doubt about something. You're not sure of the facts but you have the feeling that something or someone is not right. It is a belief you hold without proof. It is often associated with wrongdoing by someone, misplaced trust or fear. You can be suspicious yourself of someone or you can be viewed with suspicion by others.

There is an old joke that goes like this: a hitchhiker gets a lift in a car on a dark night. After a few miles, the driver turns to the hitchhiker and says, 'I'm sorry to tell you, but I am a serial axe murderer.'

The hitchhiker looks shocked and replies, 'No, you're not! What are the chances of two of us being in the same car at the one time?' They both laugh and drive on.

We do go on with suspicious minds. People often fear losing something more than they prize gaining something. In moments of uncertainty, the feeling of suspicion arises faster than trust. Suspicion is fast-tracked through the body while trust is slow-wired.

It is prudent to be on the lookout for sneaky dealings, but if you become overly wary, some of life's great opportunities and adventures can pass you by.

Suspicion is similar to jealousy in that once it enters your life it is like a parasite that bloats as it feeds itself. Suspicion is a very poor collector of objective evidence. It blinds people to looking at things through different perspectives.

Here we see the dangers of the binary brain. Your brain really wants to keep life simple. Its main objectives are to stay alive, find shelter and food and mate. To achieve this, it divides things into two choices: here or there, now or then, real or fake, true or false and us or them (which, as we have seen, is the basis of sexism, racism and most forms of violence).

Binary thinking (yes/no, this/that, here/then, us/them) gives us the luxury of fast decision-making. While this is speedy, it is not always accurate and not always true. However, in its rush, it runs the risk of grossly oversimplifying matters. Very few options and even fewer people are truly all good or all bad.

Physical signs of suspicion

- an index finger placed vertically against the cheek bone under the eye
- compressed lips
- eyebrows arched
- perplexed expression
- unsettled, agitated
- narrowed eyes
- shading eyes with hands (to help you focus on the source of your wariness)
- alert and focused.

What you may notice

Suspicion is often felt as an all-or-nothing feeling. You are either suspicious or you are not.

Feeling suspicious is a powerfully self-confirmatory emotion. Doubts linger and deepen. You begin to see what you want to see. Suspicion can convince you of something and then you automatically begin to find evidence to support your theory. Have you ever had the thought, 'I think this person is avoiding me,' and then immediately noticed things you hadn't seen before that support your thought? If you let suspicion dominate, it will override other explanations, such as the possibility that the person you think is avoiding you may be ill, shy or just plain busy.

What happens

Suspicion is a fear of losing control. It is a fear that you might be taken advantage of or taken for a ride. Suspicion can lead you to behaviours that you would not normally do, such as checking other people's phones, diaries, social media postings, computers or emails. This can become obsessive if left unchecked. Checking behaviours are attempts to regain control.

A classic example of suspicion is found in a game theory exercise called the Prisoner's Dilemma. Imagine that you and an accomplice are arrested for a crime. Both of you are placed in different rooms and can't communicate with each other. The police don't have enough evidence to charge you with a major crime, but they could charge you with a minor one, and if you are found guilty, you will serve one year in prison. The police tell you that if you inform on your accomplice, your sentence will be reduced. Unbeknown to you, they make the same offer to your accomplice.

There are four possible outcomes:

1. Both of you refuse to inform on the other and you both serve one year (demonstrates mutual trust).
2. You each inform on the other and both of you serve two years (demonstrates suspicion).
3. You inform on your accomplice, who remains silent. You walk free; they serve three years (demonstrates suspicion on your part).
4. Your accomplice informs on you while you remain silent. You serve three years while they walk free (demonstrates suspicion on your accomplice's part).

When this scenario is given once, it is optimal to inform on your accomplice. However, when it is repeated on many occasions and the two people are in an ongoing relationship, which mirrors most real-life relationships more accurately, it shows that most people would prefer collaboration and trust to suspicion.

So what does this mean for your business, personal and romantic relationships? Should you be suspicious or not?

With people you interact with once or only rarely, some guardedness is warranted. However, what makes this trickier is that you can never be certain who may pop up in your life again and again. While it would lovely to think that all your friends and associates will have your back 100 per cent of the time in an 'I will die for you' kind of way, it is unlikely.

For people you have ongoing relationships with, the ideal relationship is one based on collaboration and forgiveness. So a few questions to consider might be:

- Do I trust that the person in general has my best interests at heart?
- Do I think there could be times when their best interests and my best interests conflict with one another?
- Do I think there will be occasions when they do not have my best interests at heart?
- Do I gain support from this person?
- Do I feel that some transgressions, where their interests dominate over my interests, should determine how I relate to this person?

What you can do that helps

Some level of suspicion is healthy, especially when you are dealing with people you have never met before or you have only met occasionally. However, you don't want to be suspicious of people you have important relationships with, such as romantic or business partners, work colleagues or family members. Suspicion can dramatically alter the dynamics of these relationships and some might never recover.

Tending towards suspicion can also mean you may miss out on some opportunities in life.

It is hard to talk yourself out of suspicion. You may need to get some professional help with this. Also, be careful of spending too much time with emotionally wounded friends who, while being caring and well-meaning, can share their own history of distrust and disappointments and unwittingly influence you.

If you find suspicion is becoming more dominant in your daily life, you need to acknowledge your fears and stop any checking behaviours you may have adopted. You don't need evidence; you need a decision that leads to action. It takes courage to act on suspicion but action is always better than a life of unhappiness and unease.

If you find you tend towards being suspicious, you can channel your talents into becoming an adept reader of people. People can conceal their intentions, consciously or unconsciously, and learning how to read and recognise this is helpful. Some of these are included in the Index of Physical Signs at the end of this book. For a more complete account you might like to read Joe Navarro's book *What Every Body is Saying*. Being able to pinpoint whether someone is being genuine or not will relieve you of the burden of having to be suspicious of everyone all the time.

The suspicious brain

Suspicion relates to two regions of the brain: the amygdala, which is responsible for processing fear and emotional memories, and the parahippocampal gyrus, which is associated with putting into words what you know. How suspicious we feel depends on a baseline level of trust we have developed of people in general, and the social context at hand, both of which have strong correlations with the amygdala. When we feel suspicious, our parahippocampal gyrus becomes highly activated and acts almost like an inborn lie detector, according to a study conducted by the Virginia Tech Carilion Research Institute.

Trauma

Shocked, Fearful, Anxious, Changeable

Reactive, Stressed, Vigilant

'Traumatised people chronically feel unsafe inside their bodies. The past is alive in the form of gnawing interior discomfort. Their bodies are constantly bombarded by visceral warning signs and, in an attempt to control these processes, they often become expert at ignoring their gut feelings and in numbing awareness of what is played out inside. They learn to hide from their selves.'
– Bessel A van der Kolk, *The Body Keeps the Score*

Trauma involves experiencing high levels of stress or fear from an event that is unpredictable in nature and overwhelms us. The event is usually so nasty it is like receiving a deep punch to the brain. Usually we are not able to make sense of what is happening to us at the time. Although we can leave a traumatic situation, it may not leave us, and the effects of trauma can reverberate throughout our lives.

What you may notice

Often when we think of trauma we think of big, nasty events involving violence, abuse and neglect. There are also times when the onset of trauma was triggered by a small event that overwhelmed us.

One clue to detecting trauma is to consider times when you reacted to something in a way that seemed unusually sensitive, dramatic or reactive compared to the way you normally act. Then ask yourself if that incident relates in any way to a time earlier on when you felt overwhelmed or out of control. If so, you may have some processing to do to help you understand the original event.

Another clue is weight loss or gain. If there has been a time in your life when it seemed you put on some weight and couldn't lose it, it is worth considering if it was associated with some form of trauma in your life. When people resolve past traumas they often resume healthier weight ranges.

Physical signs of trauma

- unwanted thoughts or memories
- loss of coordination
- blanking out or getting vague moments
- weight gain or loss
- disrupted sleep
- intestinal problems.
- loss of hair, skin conditions and unexplained ridges in fingernails.

What happens

None of us like to think about the bad things that have happened to us. The feeling of being traumatised is so awful that the memory resides mostly in our unconscious mind. It is thought to be stored in the cerebellum at the base of our brain as well as in every cell of our bodies.

In times of high stress, people revert to the age they were when they experienced the trauma. All of us have three different ages:

1. our age in years
2. our age in terms of our capacity to think things through and understand them
3. our emotional age.

For most people, these three ages are aligned. But for people who have experienced trauma, these three ages can be thrown out of alignment. When we function well, our three ages are fairly much the same:

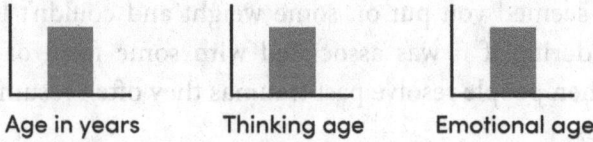

Age in years   Thinking age   Emotional age

When we are traumatised and not functioning well, our three ages become mismatched:

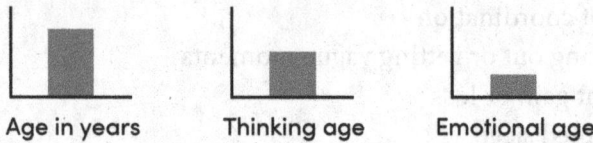

Age in years   Thinking age   Emotional age

Being out of synch in alignment like this can be perplexing for you and also completely bewildering to the other people in your life. It is why a seemingly mature, smart person can end up being a fearful crying wreck over something that seems quite straightforward to everyone else. With a traumatised child, it is also why they can seem competent and settled one moment but can suddenly resemble a much younger child the next.

Being out of whack reduces our ability to calm ourselves in stressful times, especially if those times resemble in any away the original traumatising event.

Trauma also throws our bodies out of whack. The way we move and walk can be altered. Generally, we become less coordinated and less symmetrical, because we hold the memory of the trauma in our body.

Our body's inner clock, the circadian rhythm, can also be disrupted. Sleep can be erratic or hard to achieve. Some people might find themselves up in the middle of the night pacing or cleaning or preparing. Settling down in the evening or calmly waking up in the morning can be a rarity.

Our circadian rhythms relate directly to our digestive system, so people can have issues with eating at odd hours or controlling food intake.

Some people eat very little, almost denying themselves the nourishment they need. Others deal with trauma through the comfort of food.

> **Generally, people with traumatic pasts
> don't deal with changes quickly.**

The world can be overwhelming at times for people with past trauma. This can be why some of them blank out at key moments. They can miss key details and signs. This can include the internal signs of their own feelings. One of the paradoxes of trauma is that while people can become incredibly sensitive, they are not always attuned to what their body is telling them or what they need. Generally, people with traumatic pasts don't deal with changes quickly. Shifts in circumstances are interpreted as a threat until proven otherwise. Changing rooms, rearranging the furniture or the shift from day to evening at dusk can be alarming. Throwing a surprise party for them would be tantamount to torture.

What you can do that helps

Trauma lurks in the shadows. Unprocessed and ignored, it increases in power. Bringing conscious awareness to that unconscious place is where healing can begin. The only problem is that no one likes spending time thinking about the dreadful things that have happened to them! It's upsetting.

Trauma often leaves us feeling powerless, hopeless and helpless. Often the best place to begin to deal with these feelings is with the body, as it tends to hold on to traumatic memories much more vividly than your conscious mind does. Below are some things you can do to help you start processing your trauma.

- Move at the speed of need. This will vary. Some days you will be full of pep and energy; other days you may resemble a sloth on long-service leave. Live at your own pace.

- Try a range of movement-based activities, such as yoga, Pilates, dance and swimming. Exercise of any kind can help to realign bodies and lives thrown out of whack.

- Complete a body audit. Where in your body do you feel strong? Where do you feel vulnerable? Where are you hurting? Treat any physical ailments. Try to maintain a balanced diet and don't go overboard with alcohol, cigarettes, junk food or any stress-related behaviour that makes you more upset with yourself.

- Turn the volume down! Repeatedly exposing yourself to negative news, social media feeds and conversations can be traumatising. Have at least some time each week when you access only positive news and discoveries.

- As much as possible, do something each day that you would normally do if you were feeling hopeful and calm.

- Find your own strengths and the strengths of others. Completing the Life Map in my book *Your Best Life at Any Age* is one way to begin to reflect on your strengths and to use them to create resilience at different stages of life. Completing the analysis at www.mylearningstrengths.com may also be of benefit.

- Beauty is an antidote to hopelessness. It lurks in the small details of life: the smile from a stranger, the wag of a dog's tail or a sunny morning. Search for these details. Also, intentionally create more beauty in your world for others to discover. Cherish what you can.

- It has been a hard time but let's not make it any harder than it needs to be. We tend to tell ourselves one story and make all the facts confirm that position. But is there a more helpful story we can use? For example, are we seeing around us examples of great caring and bravery, of times when people cooperate rather than clash? Have we beaten enemies and challenges in the past? Can we beat them again?

If we obsess on our trauma, it can be hard to shake off. Even worse, we can become a compliant victim rather than actively contributing to a better future for ourselves. Be a gatherer of possibility rather than a passive acceptor of a dire outcome.

Finding someone skilled and trustworthy to talk to will also be of benefit. Take it slowly. The aim is to gently peel back the layers so you can see the patterns of your life and how they have been affected by trauma. Don't rush this process, as you could re-traumatise yourself.

Trust

Sincere, Reliable, Dependable, Likeable, Supportive, Integrity, Honourable

Assured, Confident, Creative, Bold, Appreciative

'Trust is like a mirror, you can fix it if it's broken, but you can still see the crack in that mother f****r's reflection.'

– Lady Gaga

Trust entails holding a belief in someone or something that can't be shaken. It is based on the knowledge that someone is truthful and has integrity. It is a feeling that is central to all our relationships.

What you may notice

Friendship allows us to move along pathways that we could never travel alone. What enables friendships to occur is trust. When we are with people we trust we almost heave a sigh of relief. Trust is a homecoming. We think, 'Here is someone I can let my guard down with and be truly me.' We seek these people out and return again and again to spend time with them.

Trust is the foundation stone of all our relationships. Ideally your upbringing enabled you to thrive in a warm, responsive relationship that became the cradle of your sense of trust and security.

If that wasn't the case, the risk is you will be desperate enough to misplace your trust in those who will let you down. We all do this from time to time. For some of us, being let down by people becomes a heartbreaking, dispiriting pattern.

Trust is the reason we are all here. In order for you to exist, your ancestors had to survive. They survived by trusting other people enough to form tribes. If they hadn't done that, you wouldn't have been born.

We live in a world that often applauds the rugged individualist and the hardened competitor. But it was the collaborators that won, not the guy who said, 'I'm going to go off and fight that mammoth or sabre-toothed tiger by myself.' He often didn't return.

We are wired to trust. We are so wired to trust, we do it without even thinking about it. Any time you have ridden in a train, eaten out, flown in a plane or caught a taxi or uber you trusted someone you barely knew without even thinking about it. This is how wired we are to trust.

Physical signs of trust

- fiddling with hair with palm facing out exposing the underside of arms and wrists
- standing with feet crossed
- running fingers through hair
- ventilating hair (lifting hair away from the back of the neck)
- carefree in conversation
- upturned eyebrows
- faces that look happy even when they are not smiling
- direct eye contact.

What happens

Our desire to trust places us in a dilemma. To blindly trust others is to risk being duped, damaged or hurt, but not trusting leaves us lonely, anxious and insecure.

Trust is an act of bravery. It seems we often use a number of key criteria to assess the trustworthiness of someone else:

1. Do they seem credible? Are the details they share about their life plausible? We are usually skilled detectors of inauthenticity.
2. Are they reliable? Do they show up when they say they will? Can they leave when they say they will or do they hang around?
3. Do they seem open? People can be private but when someone is overly concealing about details of their life, suspicious rise.
4. Are they caring? Can they listen as well as share information?

5. Are they reciprocators? Is there a to and fro to their contribution?
6. Are they able to see differences? Can they accept that people might like or want different things or do they insist that everyone should do things their way?

While it seems sensible to advise taking your time to get to know someone before trusting them, we do tend to make snap decisions about people. (For more on this, see the section on Suspicion on page 211.)

Even the best checklist is never going to guarantee you won't be let down by people. Agreements, priorities and circumstances change. When those changes occur in our relationship with someone we have relied upon and trusted, we feel hurt and disappointed.

At these times, there is a choice to either retaliate or repair. Repair where you can but it is generally better to move on rather than waste time trying to get back at them.

More relationships fall apart from fractured trust than from boredom or incompatibility. We can all benefit from increasing our ability to repair relationships and rebuild trust.

What you can do that helps

In the earlier section on Fear, we discussed perception and neuroception. Neuroception is your gut feeling, your intuition or your inner spider sense. You've experienced this. Just as you have met people you almost instantly trusted, there are others who make your inner alarm bells ring.

Your neuroception is not always correct. Sometimes you can feel wary about someone initially, only to later feel reassured and suspect that you were overly guarded. Nevertheless, it is always important to heed your neuroception. It may get it wrong from time to time, but trust its early signalling.

Trusting the wrong people

The only way to never be let down by someone would be to trust no one. While trusting no one may seem like a solution, it often increases your vulnerability. Having decided to trust no one, people often meet someone and just fall head over heels in trust with them. All wariness and consideration go out the window.

I want to demonstrate why you should be careful. If you asked me to help you appear to be more trustworthy, there are a number of strategies I could teach you. These would include smiling more often, leaning in, looking people in the eye, nodding when they speak, and repeating key phrases they use in conversation when you speak back to them. Don't give the message that anyone else is more important. That means no fidgeting with phones or taking calls. I would also help you to mirror the other person's posture and movements.

All of these strategies are designed to highlight the similarities between people. People yearn to meet someone just like them. Someone who shares their values and world view. Someone who gets them.

So a few guidelines as we move on our way towards trust:

- Not everyone who is caring is trustworthy.
- Watch out for people who move too fast in relationships or promise too much.
- If it smells too good to be true, it probably is.
- If someone can't hear it when you say no, walk away. Generally, give people three chances. Less, if it seems dire.
- Be wary of people who repeatedly want to know where you are when you are not with them.
- Rely more on what people do than what they say they do.
- One of the best predictors of future actions is past actions so if someone has a history of betraying friends, be careful.

If you have a history of trust littered with letdowns, cheating, lying and deception, 'fess up that you are a lousy judge of who to trust. Find a wing man or wing woman who is a good judge of character to help you.

If you don't even trust yourself

Good! You shouldn't anyway. Of the 70,000 or so thoughts most people have each day, 99 per cent are on high-rotation repeat. They are thoughts that you have had before and, most likely, will have again. Many of those thoughts should be dispensed with. Learn to question your thoughts and feelings rather than trusting and believing them. By being more questioning about the validity of thoughts and feelings, you become more discerning about which ones to trust.

This is why learning about your feelings, increasing your discernment about them and knowing how to evaluate them will help you to remain sane in this crazy world.

How to swim with sharks

At some point in their lives, most people find themselves in a situation where they can trust no one. This seems to occur most frequently in work places. Don't confuse a work place with a substitute family. These are your work colleagues not your bosom buddies.

This is an opportunity to find constructive ways to work with people that rely on what they do rather than what they say they are going to do. It is also an opportunity for you to become the boss of your career, rather than expecting someone else to do it for you.

The trusting brain

We are such social creatures that we love to trust. It delights us when we feel accepted and connected to others. When people are with those they trust, they show increased activity of the ventral striatum (responsible for reward processing and positive feelings) and the medial pre-frontal cortex (responsible for decision-making and retrieving memories).

Vulnerability

Humility, Courage, Self-deprecation, Kind, Strength, Honest, Real, Grounded

Wounded, Accepting, Fearful, Human, Avoidant

'Vulnerability sounds like truth and feels like courage.
Truth and courage aren't always comfortable,
but they're never weakness.'

– Brené Brown

Being authentic and honest makes you vulnerable. We are all a mosaic of areas of competency and capability, and also of ineptitudes and limitations. Your own mix of these is yours alone. No one else shares the exact same pattern as you.

What you may notice

We launch ourselves into life trying to achieve a fairly believable cover story, promoting our best qualities while doing our darnedest to keep people from discovering our flaws. On no account should other people get to see our real self. We even think we get away with it … for a time.

Bringing all of the different aspects of yourself into some form of awareness and integration is the pathway towards self-acceptance and self-kindness.

This is gutsy work.

There are times when it is hard to be in the world. We feel exposed; open to criticism, judgment, vilification. So we put on armour for protection. Armour might look like playing the good girl/boy role; being the smart one; striving to be the fastest/strongest/prettiest; feigning disinterest and adopting an 'I'm too cool to care' visage that ends in cynicism; or joining in the torrid race to be one of the rich and famous. Look good and avoid looking bad at all costs!

The armour that protects us also inflates our ego and helps us avoid the discomfort/fear that we will be found not good enough in some way. We avoid as much as possible. What we fear is weakness. At its heart is a deep understanding that our communities can be competitive and dangerous, and we need protection from attack. At the same time, the armour we hide behind inhibits authentic relationships – with ourselves and others. It diminishes the joy and richness of connecting in an open and real way with those we love and work with. So how do we walk this line?

**Looking good, or at least attempting to do so,
can ruin our lives.**

Looking good, or at least attempting to do so, can ruin our lives. We view mistakes not as learning opportunities but as punishable offences. If someone sees us before a certain hour without make-up or styled hair we can be mortified. Heaven forbid that the house could be messy, the kids less than brilliant and that our relationship could have even a minor hint of an issue. If we trip in the street, our first concern may not be whether we are injured but whether anyone saw us.

It is odd that most people can happily tell you that they are crazy busy but if you pause and ask them if they are having trouble coping, they will hotly deny it.

What happens

Our avoidance of vulnerability is amplified by living in a world where everyone is supposed to be extraordinary. Be a winner. Be elite. Be gifted. Be in the top percentage of people who … (fill in the blank).

This is a form of dominance behaviour where some people assert they are especially important because they are part of a higher-level of clique. In this world view, it is not enough to be successful; it is also necessary to have everyone else envy your success. Is a holiday that doesn't make other people seethe with envy really a holiday at all?

We could enter a weird fake race where my fake self competes with your fake self to have more of a fake good time than your fake good time. Or perhaps it is time to 'fess up. To be honest. Authentic.

To avoid feeling vulnerable we invest a lot of time in building our defences, looking good, looking successful. Avoiding any signs of weakness. Ironically, it is all this avoidance that increases our fear of vulnerability. In addition to being inauthentic, it traps us into being conventional. When you are keeping up with the Joneses you are not keeping up with yourself.

There is an interesting kind of quirky paradox contained in all of this. The people who may be the most intriguing are the ones who are brave enough to be themselves and embrace their vulnerabilities. These are the true free radicals.

One of the major afflictions caused by our failure to accept our vulnerabilities is the crippling sense of body shame.

What you can do that helps

Let's be blunt. We are all bags of bacteria and squishy blood and organs encased in this attractive package of skin. We all pee, poo, fart, burp, have wobbly bits, droopy bits, bits that are too large and bits that are too small. Most of us would prefer that no one else ever gets to see these bits. And that's just the physical side of things. Add in the reality that we can all be snitchy, grumpy, bitchy, nasty, greedy, aggressive and conniving and we are going to need some serious cover work to get away with this.

Look at the industries that profit from people's desire to conceal the 'awful' truth from others – weight loss, gyms, teeth whitening, photoshopping, plastic surgery, shapewear, liposuction, perfumes, hair transplants, beauty products, air fresheners – and you begin to see that this mission consumes a fair proportion of human endeavour and income.

So what does this mean in practical terms? Well, it doesn't mean you need to greet every newcomer with a list of your deficits and shortcomings. Imagine a date that began with one person saying, 'Now, before anything happens let me tell you how truly awful I can be.' Nor does it mean that you should adopt a 'You need to accept me warts and all' approach to social relationships. This is not a licence to be crass or boorish or inconsiderate.

If you can be brave enough to become vulnerable you become brave enough to be yourself.

Accepting, even exulting in our vulnerabilities means being courageous enough and open-hearted enough to our whole self and to being able to accept others for who they truly are.

If you can be brave enough to become vulnerable and let others see it, you become brave enough to be yourself.

Wonder and awe

Awestruck, Curiosity, Appreciation, Soothed, Admiration, Spellbound, Transfixed

Naïve, Fearful, Shocked, Gleeful, Animated, Ecstatic

*'The world is full of magic things waiting for our
senses to grow sharper.'*

– WB Yeats

Wonder is fleeting but misery is enduring. We can sustain moroseness and bad moods for hours and sometimes days on end. Some people almost seem to make a lifestyle out of it. They have the anti-Midas touch: whatever they touch turns to excrement.

Wonder, on the other hand, catches you on the hop. Before you know it you are admiring a bird in flight, spellbound by a sunset or luxuriating in freshly laundered sheets. Wonder is transient. It is discovered in the small fleeting moments.

What you may notice

One of the greatest gifts children give adults is reconnecting them with the feelings of wonder and awe. The shimmering of a cobweb that catches the light or the delight of splashing in a puddle – childhood at its best is a forest of first encounters. When we live in wonder we seek treasures. It is a gateway to gratitude.

Unlike surprise or shock, where there is an initial constriction of the senses, wonder creates an expansion of sensation and awareness.

It is easy to be a complacent know-it-all. The world seems able to reduce the most wonderful things to bland familiarity bordering on contempt, and it is easy to become jaded.

For adults, it is easy to see things in terms of comparisons. Often this causes a diminishment in themselves. For example, they might express the sentiment that: 'I could never paint that', 'run that fast', 'leap that far' or 'speak in public that clearly'. This is admiration mixed with envy.

Wonder is the sense of being awed by something without being diminished by it. If you have ever watched the sweep of stars on a clear night or heard the opening of Mozart's 'Symphony No. 9' or glimpsed two people in love looking at each other, you will know this.

What happens

The fleeting nature of a shooting star is a good analogy for wonder. Its brevity means we don't get a chance to tire of it. We remain dazzled.

We are always just an imagination away from wonder. Often we need to distract ourselves in order to catch it.

To paraphrase the thoughts of Nikos Kazantzakis, what a strange creation humans are. You fill them with bread, wine, fish and radishes and out of them come sighs, dreams and laughter.

Wonder and its expression in poetry and the arts are among the most important things that seem to distinguish people from other animals, and intelligent and sensitive people from morons.

Every day we are surrounded by the miraculous, but we seem determined not to see it. We are aware of only a minuscule fragment of the world. Of the 11,000,200,000 bits of information that assail or entice our senses every second, we only consciously process 77.

What you can do that helps

Take time to notice. Beyond the world of comparison between your ego and its achievements sit the most magnificent wonders.

Actively bring more wonder into your life. Make soup. Brew up some kombucha or ginger beer. Grow a garden. Arrange flowers. Enjoy the seasons. Watch for absurdity. Enjoy the weather, whatever it is. (Unless you have some special weather-changing powers, you might as well.)

Go on a hunt for the golden treasures of life. Start with a search for beauty.

How to be awed by a loved one

Most of us forget to really learn about the people we are with. That is especially true of our loved ones. Start getting curious about them. Make it a practice to ask them one unusual question about themselves a couple of times a week.

Some ways are:

- Pretend to yourself that you are meeting them for the first time and get to know them afresh.
- Ask them questions like what is the best piece of music they have ever heard or what was their most cherished toy as a child.
- Decide that you are lucky to know them.

Be in the wonder of a child

A child's spirit is like a blossoming garden. New shoots are spreading in all directions. Their minds are like popcorn – just add a catalyst and you can't be sure which direction they are going to bounce in. Revel in their joy and try to replicate it if you can for yourself.

Be alone and in wonder

Look to the skies. Go to an art gallery or a musical performance. Combine the most delicious ingredients you can to make a mouth-watering dish. Walk along a street and imagine yourself being an enthusiastic sports commentator, documenting your every step.

Turn on a tap; water comes out. Flick a switch; light comes on. You have access to things even the richest people of past times couldn't have even dreamed of. It doesn't have to be huge or exciting. The magic is in the small things.

Choose to be lucky

Remember you are the beneficiary of your ancestors. All of those good people who, for at least 1.5 million years, have helped you to be here.

Most of them are no longer with us. As far as we know they can no longer do any of the things that you can do.

Awe and the brain

Awe seems to pull us out of ourselves and make us feel immersed in our surroundings and the larger world.

Little is known about the neurological mechanisms that underlie the awe experience. One small study, conducted among people who were in simulated space flight, found differences in two types of brain waves – theta and beta – between people who did and did not experience awe.

Worry and anxiety

Concern, Careful, Hesitant, Cautious, Belonging, Sharing, Humility

Anxious, Fearful, Anguish, Timorous, Terrified, Ruminative

'Anxiety is the interest paid on trouble before it is due.'
– William Ralph Lace

Worrying is the state of being troubled or concerned over an actual situation or a potentially problematic situation. It is related closely to fear because the outcome is uncontrollable and uncertain. And as we know, our brains like certainty. Worry can be useful in pointing out situations where we need to be careful but it can also become a dominant way of thinking that has negative consequences for our lives.

What you may notice

If worries just visited us once, they wouldn't be an issue. If we could just think to ourselves, 'Oh, I'm worrying about (insert any issue you can think of)' and that was the end of it, all would be okay. The trouble is, worries are such insistent pests. They move into our heads, make a lot of noise and want to rearrange all the furniture. Attention seeking? More like attention demanding.

Worrying is not the same as caring. It is not the same as solving a problem. It is like spinning the wheels on a car and going nowhere fast.

The people we worry about are no better off for our efforts. Worrying is a largely useless activity, unlike caring and kindness. We live in a world that appears addicted to worrying but feels paralysed to do anything about it. We might use a mindfulness app or do deep breathing or try to silence our minds, but we don't do much to ease out of the worrying addiction itself.

Worrying by yourself can be a sleepless, repetitive, circular activity, but a worry shared is a worry amplified. Worrying is quite literally loopy thinking.

Worrying is also like an infectious disease. It is easily spread and its offshoots, fear and alarm, have found the perfect landing place in social and local media. For example, it is often difficult to tell where worrying ends and where the real news begins. News shows today are filled with disturbing images, often packaged with music and headlines signalling urgency and alarm. They no longer tell just local stories. Instead they share grisly and gruesome events from across the world. Modern news can be information anxiety.

Over-connected and hyper-vigilant

In our hyper-wired culture, if we don't hear back from a friend within a few hours, we start worrying that the friendship may have ended. In fact, it is now considered downright rude if you leave someone hanging when you read their text or direct message and don't reply immediately. You have left them on 'read'. This act can spark a whole range of paranoia and suspicion. (See section on Suspicion.) If parents don't hear back from their children within nanoseconds they can hyperventilate.

The expectations of faster responses have risen but the expectations of the quality of work have not decreased. Nor has there been an expansion of free time to deal with email, texts and social media postings.

In a time when everyone's opinion seems to be given equal weight, we can be perplexed by a myriad of perspectives and no longer feel certain of the truth. We have more choice and can suffer from a sense of analysis paralysis. We live in a world where people are continually on 'jury duty' and feel compelled to judge, like or comment on issues on social media.

Alvin Toffler predicted the rate of change would overwhelm humans in his 1970 book *Future Shock*, but at over 500 pages in length, these days we lack the time and attention span to read it.

Young people check their phones on average about 150 times a day. It takes us on average 23 minutes to regain our focus after an interruption. Are we seeing a link with feeling time-poor?

What happens

All of us have an internal commentary that appraises our actions. Is your internal voice that of an understanding friend or of a harsh critic?

Most people don't relate as much to the external world as they do to their own internal world. In this sense, all of us have an internal audience that we speak to and who appraise our actions. Whether someone's internal audience is full of positive barrackers or negative deriders plays a powerful role in their lives.

Worrying is often the concerned or negative internal audience taking prominence in a person's life. It is usually a splitting of the self into two:

1. There is the 'good' self who wants to improve, perform and function; and
2. The 'bad' self who is flawed and needs to take a long, hard look at themselves, and start improving.

As hard as the 'good' self wants to try to talk the 'bad' self into lifting their game, going on a diet, getting fitter, working more productively or saving more money, the 'bad' self resents such bossiness, even if it is well intentioned, and wants to tell the good self to go and find someone else to annoy.

Of course, if the 'good' self was able to really talk the 'bad' self into becoming perfect, then you would become the sort of self-righteous prig that no one could stand being around and that would most likely give you something else to worry about.

Now the problem with worry is that it is so damn useful.

Worry then is a sort of buck-you-up pep talk. The problem, of course, is while we are focused on giving ourselves a severe talking to, we aren't really living life. You can't really be in a race and commenting on the race at the same time.

Life is not neat. In even the luckiest lives accidents happen, mistakes occur, plans go wildly astray and illnesses and frailties wait. What keeps us from happiness is our inability to fully inhabit the present.

We use our minds to retreat into our minds. We make plans and schemes, evaluate, judge, assess and generally become fixated with a whirlpool of ideas, predictions and worries. This is why the world rushes about enjoying only small momentary fragments of existence. It is when we lose ourselves that we are most likely to feel ecstatic.

The world is largely focused on measuring and counting. It does not value experiences or biological rhythms much.

We live then for a future that may or may not happen. We invest so much worry into the uncertainties of our future because we value control more than we value happiness, and they are largely mutually exclusive.

Now the problem with worry is that it is so damn useful. It kept your ancestors alive so they could produce you. It really is a valuable signal. However, when it dominates everything else, it becomes a detriment to enjoying life. So you need to find ways to turn it on and to turn it off.

What you can do that helps

Recognising and understanding your own individual response to worry and anxiety means you will have a better chance of not getting unnecessarily worried and stressed, or will be better at worrying for shorter periods of time. It is simple; it's just not easy. Let's look at the three main ways we worry or are affected by worry and some ways to mitigate them.

Freeze

We sometimes talk about people being scared stiff, shocked speechless or like a rabbit frozen in the headlights. The freeze response is hardwired into our brains. It is our most primitive survival strategy.

Sometimes in the face of threat we dissociate from the here and now. This is when you literally lose all sense of yourself in the moment. Your mind feels like it has gone somewhere else. You are stuck and immobile. If you can't make the threat disappear, you're much better off disappearing yourself.

Dissociating from an event vastly beyond your capacity to handle it is a good strategy as a child but can become frustratingly maladaptive as an adult. However, there is something we can try to deal with this habit of freezing, which I have outlined below.

A quick trip to vagus

Our tenth cranial nerve, the vagus nerve, is the main conduit between our brain and body. It soothes us and keeps us in the resilient mindset. It helps us to gently apply the brakes and recover after stress.

The vagus nerve tells the brain what's going on in our organs, including the stomach and intestines, lungs and heart, spleen, liver and kidneys. It impacts on eye contact, facial expressions and our ability to tune in to other people's voices.

The higher our vagal tone (the synching between our heart rate and our rate of breathing) the better. This increases the efficiency of our heart, breath by breath.

We all have variability in our vagal tone. When we breathe in, our heart rate increases slightly and when we breathe out, our heart rate lowers. This is why deep breathing or belly breathing, using slow extended breaths out, calms us down. How many times have you heard someone tell a distressed or panicked person to take a deep breath? There is a reason for it!

Some of us have stronger vagus activity, which means our bodies can relax faster after a stress.

People with higher vagal tones are able to regulate their internal body processes (ie calm themselves down) more efficiently and are generally more flexible in their ability to do this. This makes them more agile in their ability to focus on their surroundings and recognise any opportunities or dangers.

Some of us have stronger vagus activity, which means our bodies can relax faster after a stress. The stronger your vagal tone is, the stronger your body is at regulating blood glucose levels, which reduces the likelihood of diabetes, stroke and cardiovascular disease.

One of the vagus nerve's jobs is to reset the immune system and switch off production of proteins that fuel inflammation. The main neurotransmitter involved in this process is acetylcholine, which is also related to the process of learning. Two important reasons why we need to shape up our vagus nerve!

How we can all improve our vagal tone

Exercises to increases vagal tone include:

- slow breathing – by deep belly breathing, you alter the way your brain stem signals to the diaphragm to contract
- practising self-kindness
- singing or chanting with others
- hugging
- eating well and taking probiotics to keep our gut flora stable and healthy
- having cold showers
- reducing jaw tension
- reducing neck tension
- rubbing the back of your neck or behind your ears gently
- splashing your face with cold water
- laughter
- play
- hand warming
- feeling and showing love and appreciation.

Oh no, I have frozen! What now?

1. Notice the freeze. This is a feeling of being immobilised and stuck.
2. Know the freeze is temporary.
3. Breathe slowly.
4. As you come out of a freeze, you may feel exhausted. Sometimes after we freeze we tell ourselves we are sad, lazy or not coping, rather than just recognising we need to rest.
5. As you tune back into your body, accept any feelings and any movements that occur. For example, you may shake, tremble or have goosebumps. This is old energy leaving your body.

Fight or flight

When we experience excessive worry and anxiety our body prepares for running or fighting. The fight-or-flight system bypasses our rational mind and moves us into survival mode. Non-essential services (ie digestion or building an immune system) are switched off. Our body is geared up for action. This is the time to run it out, walk it out, sing it out, or dance it out. Just move.

If we don't rid ourselves of the build-up of hormones that accompany worry and anxiety we are in trouble. Cortisol floating around our body for too long is like an out-of-control delinquent looking for trouble.

If we retain high levels of cortisol and adrenaline in our body for too long we can experience a range of symptoms, such as:

- Headache/migraine
- Irritable bowel syndrome
- High blood pressure
- Chronic fatigue
- Depression
- Eye twitching
- Teeth-grinding.

Connect, protect, respect

Another way people can deal with worry is called connect, protect, respect and has to do with the release of oxytocin.

Oxytocin is the bonding love drug that is released into our brain from our hypothalamus when we hug, touch, talk and interact with people. Being in synch calms us down, increases feelings of trust and decreases fear.

The connect, protect, respect routine involves doing activities with other people, looking after others in times of stress and befriending those around you to increase the likelihood of survival. Oxytocin counteracts the effects of the stress response in the body.

Worry and the brain

When we worry, our brain goes into a loop. We tend to worry about the same things over and over again. This is a called ruminative worrying and is also associated with brooding.

Not surprisingly, if both continue for some time, we are more likely to feel sad and depressed. Two parts of the brain that seem to be especially involved in this situation are the dorso-lateral pre-frontal cortex (DLPFC) which, among others things, helps to weigh up the pros and cons of alternatives, and the anterior cingulate gyrus, which plays a role in helping us detect different contexts and alter our actions accordingly.

Simply put, this leaves us with having fewer thoughts in general and those we do have we mull over and over again. It also makes us less inclined to change what we do about an issue. All in all, this is not the best recipe for flexible problem-solving. Add cortisol and adrenaline to the mix and we also see an increase in the bodily signs of stress.

Worthlessness and self-loathing

Self-deprecation, Disgust, Projection, Blame, Envy, Damnation, Self-harm, Self-hatred

Denigration, Harshness, Critical, Immobilised, Fearful, Trepidation, Denigration

'In times of peace the war-like person attacks themselves.'
– Frederick Nietzsche

To rob anyone of their worth is a crime. To steal your own worth is a personal tragedy.

What you may notice

Self-loathing is a breakdown of your relationship with yourself. It is a cold and clinical self-laceration. You have selective inattention, meaning you can only see the worst of yourself and none of your best aspects.

Self-hatred is the most dangerous disease humans can have. It can kill you. People with self-loathing and ingrained feelings of inadequacy are not open to contrary evidence. Their inner judge is harsh and severely punishing. The defence counsel has disappeared and the judge is unwilling to consult the jury.

If you met your self-hating self at a social event, you would probably think you have just spent time with a self-pitying, self-centred, fixated person with a giant chip on their shoulder. And you might just be right. However, it is more probable that you did not meet them at a social function at all: self-haters typically do great cover-up jobs. Some of them can be life-of-the-party jokesters who appear to be very comfortable in their own skins. Away from the social spotlight, however, the self-disgust gnaws away.

243

For self-haters, the adage 'Love your neighbour as yourself' would be a recipe for war.

Nietzsche's quote on the previous page shows that behind self-loathing is the act of comparison. The comparisons we make between ourselves and others, regardless of whether they are favourable or negative, cost us. They rob us of living our own lives. Behind comparison sits woundedness.

Most self-loathers come from a long line of self-loathers. It is a curse that gets passed down from one generation to the next.

What happens

Nursing the idea secretly that, within yourself, there is something monstrous, detestable and dreadful, is hard to bear. More young women than young men tend to regard themselves as worthless. While all of us have some moments of self-doubt, to truly regard yourself as worthless is tragic.

Many self-haters have a sense of being a fraud. Any position of regard or responsibility that they have attained in life is seen as a matter of luck or blindness on the part of the people who promoted them. Therefore, they need to be permanently vigilant. The feeling that anyone, at any time, could see through the cover job they have so skilfully created, is fear-inducing. Sadly, the better the cover job, the worse things can get. This is almost a subset of imposter syndrome.

One cost of camouflaging yourself is hiding yourself behind a false self or persona. No one gets to know the real you. You might feel that if they did, they would dislike you intensely. As Johann Wolfgang von Goethe, a German poet, scientist and artist, is famously quoted as saying: 'If I knew myself, I would run away.'

A second cost is the suppression of your authentic self. You may set up false leads. Your social media page may be filled with smiling faces rather than depicting who you actually are. You may deride people who are able to show the world something you feel you need to conceal about yourself. You may begin to detest people who make a contribution or appear to have fulfilled lives. Inside, you may feel as if you are dying.

Some people develop behaviour patterns that stem from their feelings of worthlessness. These can range from not spending money on themselves, or not giving themselves enough rest, to punishing themselves in the form of overexercising or food deprivation, or other forms of self-sabotage.

What you can do that helps

Feelings of being worthless and self-loathing come in waves. Usually people experience times of relative calm followed by binges of loathing and intense self-denigration. There is a cyclical pattern to this. Learn these patterns. Hormonal? Situational? Sleep deprivation? Weight gain? Are they linked to particular people, situations, demands?

Start to see these cycles as part of a pattern. Acknowledging to yourself that you're going through the I-hate-myself phase right now contains within it the awareness that this, too, will change.

If you wait to feel better about yourself before changing, you will wait forever. You need to start changing what you do, and changing what you think.

From self-hate and self-loathing to kindness

Self-loathing often relates to envy. It is a form of personal stagnation where you stop growing and feel hateful and hopeless.

Stop focusing so much on how you measure up to other people. Instead, consider how you measure up to your own goals and how you've developed as a person throughout your life.

Lessen the feelings of inadequacy by being humble. Instead of humility about one's attributes and abilities, let's think about humility with respect to self-knowledge, or recognising that we don't know ourselves nearly as well as we think we do.

Show yourself some kindness

Treat yourself as you would treat a child you love. Be kind and supportive to yourself as you try to improve. If you hate yourself for mistakes you made, take action and make amends where you can.

Your life is your creation. The past is past. Your life is now your invention. Awful things may have happened in the past but now you have become your own abuser. Stop being your own bully. Instead, make a pact with yourself to be no better and also no worse than anyone else.

Make a contribution

Let's say for a moment that you are committed to seeing yourself as the most loathsome, horrible, worthless creature on the planet. You see no way of changing your sense of disgust about yourself.

If that is the case I suggest you use the great American inventor Buckminster Fuller as a role model. After a failed attempt to shorten his own life, he decided to dedicate his life to improving the lives of others.

The self-loathing brain

When we feel worthless and awful about ourselves, the same part of the brain that is involved in disgust, the insular cortex, is activated.

Because the same neural pathways in the brain are used for feelings of both love and hate, when someone is depressed the wiring along this pathway becomes weakened and contributes more heavily to feelings of self-hate. Simultaneously the ability to feel love is lessened, which contributes further to feelings of being unloved and unlovable.

Zest

Self-caring, Revitalised, Rejuvenated, Vitality, Mojo, Zip

Weary, Zonked, Gutted, Fatigued

'Give me the comma of imperfect striving, thus to find zest in the immediate living. Ever the reaching but never the gaining, ever the climbing but never the attaining of the mountain top.'

– Winston Graham

What you may notice

Full of beans. Bouncing on tippy toes. Raring to go. There are times when we feel ready for anything. Even though these times may be fleeting, it is always worth building a nest for their arrival.

If you have ever been to a garden nursery and bought a plant, it is likely that the plant came with some instructions that outlined its optimal growing conditions, such as, 'Plant in partial shade and provide plenty of water for optimal growth.'

We are like that plant. We also have optimal growing conditions. These are the conditions under which we thrive rather than merely survive.

Consider what these might be for you. They are not the same for everyone. The amount of sleep you need to feel zestful will be different than it is for other people. It is okay; you need what you need. This is about allowing your body's energy to guide you.

If you provide your body with the nourishment and nurturance it needs to be zestful, you can't go far wrong.

For some people, optimal growing conditions involve lots of socialising; for others, times of solitude. It's okay; you need what you need. Others require many things on the go at the one time to keep them firing on all cylinders while others perform best on one task alone. It's okay; you need what you need.

The poet David Whyte wisely says that the answer to exhaustion is not always rest; it can also be wholeheartedness. Creating a life, a family, a workplace or a purpose you can give yourself passionately and wholeheartedly to is enlivening.

The world's tendency to rush fragments purpose and meaning. People often feel split between multiple tasks and roles, feeling that they are doing none of them well. After a time, their sense of purpose dulls down and becomes secondary to the power of the to-do list.

Signs of exhaustion

- head in hands
- rubbing eyes
- tired-looking eyes
- heaving of shoulders
- disturbed sleep patterns
- lack of motivation
- loss of creativity
- jumpy, jerky movements
- teeth grinding
- increased pain sensitivity.

Zest is being full of life. The myth of Sisyphus, as outlined below, shows us what happens when we engage in meaningless drudgery and remove our hearts from what we do.

In Homer's *Odyssey*, Sisyphus is condemned to painstakingly and slowly roll a boulder up a hill, knowing that at the end of the day he would never reach the summit and the boulder would roll back down to its original position. The next day he would have to repeat the same undertaking. In the story, Sisyphus was condemned to the underworld and his futile existence can be said to mirror the pointlessness of life and the subsequent exhaustion some people feel when they don't have any zest.

In a much more modern context, traffic jams are a perfect example where a lot of people lose their zest for life! Sitting trapped in their cars, unable to move for sometimes hours on end, they can feel as if their life is, literally, going nowhere. Passion and enthusiasm for life rapidly dims.

What happens

Zest abandons us at specific times of the year. If you consider your own levels of energy over time, you will know there are certain periods when you are simply zombie-walking through the day. This is what it might be like:

You wake up. Often for the second or third time. You have slept reasonably well but you still feel weary. You slug your way out of bed reluctantly. You are not your usual sweet, lovely self. You feel like anything could send you into a tail spin.

Often this is in late winter when vitamin D levels might be depleted. You trudge your way through the day. You feel on edge. Snappier than usual. Bone tired and tetchy.

At 3 or 4 pm you crave comfort foods. Maybe earlier. Maybe all day long. The muffins call to you. Chocolate screeches its invitation. Cravings for salty and sweet snacks fill your mind.

At 6 pm you are more awake than you have been all day long. You are ready to party at the very time you should be winding down for the day. You have energy now but it's an odd, wired, frenetic kind of energy.

You try to sleep but your thoughts are racing. You may have cramps or jumpy legs in bed. This can be an indication that your body has depleted itself of magnesium and zinc due to stress.

If you normally deal with the complexities of being around other people, your adrenal glands are telling you it is time to have a rest from their dramatic intensities.

Welcome to the world of the weary warrior. Let's talk about how not to have that dominate our lives.

What you can do that helps

We arrive at wholeheartedness, in part, by identifying the core values that fuel our passions and aspirations.

Come alive

When we are exhausted, we are out of rhythm with ourselves. It is time to reconnect with nature. One way to do this, other than actually going outside, is to observe the natural rhythms of the seasons and apply them to your daily life.

The morning is a blossoming of energy and imagination and resembles the springtime and emerging energy of the day. Use this time of the day to tackle the harder parts of your job or tasks at hand.

By midday, efforts are actualised and brought into full being like summer.

After this, it is time to harvest the benefits of that work. It is the gathering-in of the day as evening draws near. Marvel at the richness of autumn. Review what you have done and get ready to call it quits.

Night is the winter of the day with a time to be still, to rest and renew. Refresh your mind by talking with friends and family while resting your body. Prioritise sleep and take naps if necessary.

> *'Don't ask what the world needs. Ask what makes you come alive, and go do it. Because what the world needs is people who have come alive.'*

– Howard Thurman

When you feel exhausted, it is a great time in life to take long-service leave without the leave. For a period of six weeks, act as if you were on long-service leave. Take time out of the wild hurly burly of life to visit friends, see movies, go on walks and catch up with yourself. As Joan Anderson recommends in her wonderful book, *A Weekend to Change Your Life*, it is a time for the Six Rs: retreat, repair, retrieve, regroup, regenerate and return.

This is more about 'won't' power than 'willpower'. Clear the to-do list and have a do-now list and a won't-do-now list.

It takes determination to step back from the maelstrom of the busy world and pause to consider the life you want to live. Switch off the computer, put your phone away, turn away from the flood of news updates, dampen the screeching voices on social media who want to inform you of their opinions about everything and take some time for you. Invite yourself to increase your levels of zest and enthusiasm and to ponder what kind of life you want for yourself.

Reduce the mental clutter. Your brain is good for thinking things. It is not so great at storing lots of minor details. Develop a system to store ideas and projects but realise you won't be at your most creative when you are weary.

I would offer the same advice here as I did in the section on Busyness and haste. As a general rule of thumb, follow the rule of the threes. Once a year, maybe more, you need at least three weeks to rest, recover and rejuvenate. Once a month you need three days on your own terms. Once a week take three hours to do something of your choosing. You can involve others but if they want to do something different during this time, let them do what they want but don't join them. Preserve this time for yourself.

Zest occurs when you plan for it.

How to stay sane in a crazy world

How does the craziness creep into our lives? Sometimes it is from inside us in the form of negative thoughts, past memories and experiences that rattle around inside our heads, on high rotation. Other times it is external toxicity from other people and the world that infiltrates us.

For much of history, our ancestors lived in times characterised by physical hardship, including variable reliability of food and medical supplies, the dangers of dentistry or childbirth as well as violence in the form of invasion or attack. These are things that do not make us yearn for the good old days. If you can turn a tap and enjoy a hot shower, flick a switch and have light, use antibiotics to treat an infection, turn an oven on and cook a meal or gain access to entertainment at a moment's notice, you have luxuries beyond even the dreams of the most wildly rich kings, queens or maharajas of past times.

The world has shifted from physical hardships to mental and emotional ones. The world is not designed to support sanity. High-sugar diets drive high-stress lifestyles, social media increases sleep deprivation and envy, social hierarchies over-emphasise comparison at the expense of self-acceptance, opinions and judgments are obstacles to kindness, low levels of trust cause anxiety and a fear of social rejection, and a loss of connection with the rhythms of nature leaves us vulnerable to sadness, alienation and, sometimes, depression.

Essentially, you want to be the beneficiary of the conveniences and best medical practices the modern world can provide while maintaining some aspects of your ancestors' lifestyles such as a low-sugar diet, frequent movement and high levels of community and social connectedness.

To cope with the bombardment of the toxic world we self-medicate with alcohol, drugs, television and food in an attempt to remain sane.

However, this often comes at a cost. We watch more cooking shows but eat more take-away food. We buy smart phones with sleep apps but become exhausted and withdrawn. We join more gyms but spend more time sitting. We feel more isolated than ever before but are too busy to spend time with friends. The first thing we turn towards in the morning is a screen.

The signs that previously indicated someone may be experiencing mental disturbance – speaking loudly to yourself in the street, staring fixedly at objects, appearing dissociated and switched off from those around you, being obsessed with the shape of your eyebrows and being unable to tolerate even the slightest delay while making negative assessments of yourself in relation to others – are the norm in many cities.

By recognising insanity in the world we can reclaim sanity in ourselves. These are a few key things to consider in doing this.

Drop envy.

Stop thinking your life only has value when measured against other people's lives, achievements, appearances, bank balances or social media profiles. Locking yourself into a world of comparing yourself to and keeping up with others destines you to being driven by dreams that are not your own. Live your own life.

Increase your awareness and refine the descriptions of your feelings

Just as a food or wine taster needs to refine the sensitivity of their taste buds, we need to finely differentiate between feelings.

Feelings are confusing and we are simple pattern-seeking beings. There is always a risk that we take one snippet of a wisp of a fragment of a sensation and convert it not only into a whole feeling but a whole pattern.

Imagine you are entering a room of people you haven't met before and you want to make a good impression. You may become aware of a sense of anticipatory alertness and a shallowness of breathing. You may even perspire slightly (an ancient way of signalling fear or anxiety to others). As someone who likes to make sense of things, you could either interpret this combination as preparation for a challenge or you could consider you are experiencing anxiety. If you make the latter interpretation, your patterned mind then kicks in and unhelpfully reminds you of other social settings in which you made a complete idiot of yourself, and you feel like running away.

That process is usually:

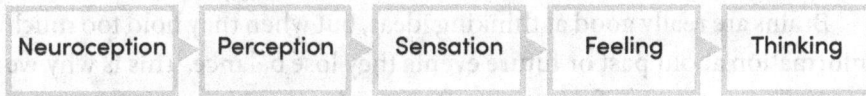

Neuroception ▷ Perception ▷ Sensation ▷ Feeling ▷ Thinking

Being able to differentiate between these states is a major advantage. Being able to question your feelings and test them for validity frees you to do the things you want.

Talk about your feelings

We often come to terms with our feelings through discussion with others. While solitary reflection is also valuable, it is often in conversations with caring people we trust that we unveil what is lurking behind a particular set of feelings.

Move your body more

Your ancestors walked somewhere between 5 and 11 kilometres a day. A body that is moving has energy and feelings flowing through it.

Your body is an information system. When it is coherent, it regulates and balances your blood pressure, heart rate, blood sugar and hormones. Your immune system functions to ward off illness. Your circulatory system oxygenates your body, promoting healing. Your digestive system converts food into energy and eliminates waste. Your nervous system alerts or calms you in accordance with your needs.

Naturally and with relative ease, your body adapts to the needs of your environment, shifting its state and balance according to demands. We are healthiest and function at our peak when we are in harmony with others but also in harmony within ourselves.

Be here now

One of the main ways our body's natural balance is thrown out of balance is when we give it signals that mislead it to believe that what's happening in our heads is more important than what's happening around us. We do this when we focus too much on the future (often causing anxiety) or too much on the past (often causing sadness, regret or bitterness) or a mix of both future and past focus (which can lead to dread and avoidance). In all of these instances we lose awareness of what is happening around us.

Brains are really good at thinking ideas, but when they hold too much information about past or future events they lose balance. This is why we need systems to get information out of our brain and into an organised system so we can focus on awareness of ourselves and our world.

Differentiate between connection and attachment

Being connected to people supports our sanity and our sense of fulfil-ment. The quality of our relationships is an essential aspect of our lives. Make a contribution to others.

Attachment is often more need-based than connection and can be less secure. There is a risk that the reliance on others through attachment can stifle some of your own development. Instead be kind, connect and, above all, be a good friend.

Don't over-generalise

Our skills at recognising patterns drive us towards generalising. This is how we get stuck. Pattern recognition can be a powerful tool, but we're prone to the binaries of good/bad and positive/negative. This is like trying to apply straight lines and right angles to a world where these do not naturally occur.

Becoming conscious of these binaries as they emerge in our thinking can lead us to either stop exploring or towards increased curiosity. Opening ourselves up to considering possibilities beyond simple either/or answers increases exploration and the opportunity for growth.

Don't back sides, back wholes

An insane world wants to divide and conquer. Its simplistic thinking sets one side against another in an endless tournament of wills. While this is fine if you are barracking for your sports team, it is not a wise thing to apply the same thinking to your life.

Look for whole gains and systems rather than part gains. Backing sides is a little like supporting the bees against the flowers in a garden, not realising that the garden needs both to survive.

Desperate to find victory, we attach ourselves to one side or the other and blind ourselves to seeing that a sane world is a diverse and tolerant one.

Love more

In a world that seems to want to dehumanise and depersonalise people, increasing the amount that we love is a revolutionary act. Be courageous, be vulnerable, love more.

Index of feelings

As feelings are complex and have multiple sources, it can be bewildering to decipher what exactly is going on. This index links a wide range of feelings with the associated feelings covered in this book.

Abhorrence – see disgust

Acceptance – see vulnerability, grief

Addiction – see desire and attraction, ambition

Admiring – see envy

Aggravated – see anger

Agitated – see anger, fear

Alert – see curiosity

Amazed – see surprise

Ambitious – see busyness and haste, betrayal, confidence, greed and possessiveness

Ambivalence – see regret, resentment, shame

Amusement – see happiness

Anger – see hate, apathy and boredom, grief

Angst – see hate

Anguish – see anger

Annoyed – see anger

Anxiety – see fear, worry and anxiety, trauma

Apathy – fear, grief, worry and anxiety, sadness

Appalled – see disgust

Appreciation – see love, kindness, equanimity

Apprehensive – see fear, suspicion

Argumentative – see anger

Arrogant – see ambition, apathy and boredom

Assured – see confidence

Attracted – see addiction, love, desire and attraction

Avaricious – see greed and possessiveness

Aversion – see disgust

Avid – see curiosity

Avoidant – see apathy and boredom, failure

Aware – see equanimity

Balanced – see equanimity

Bargaining – see grief

Bereft – see grief

Betrayal – see hate, forgiveness, greed and possessiveness

Bewildered – see ambiguity

Bitterness – see anger, regret, resentment, disappointment, disgust, hurt and heartbreak

Blaming – see failure, bitterness

Blissful – see happiness

Boastful – see ambition, envy

Bold – see courage

Brave – see courage

Brooding – see worry and anxiety, resentment

Burned out – see ambition

Busyness and haste – see ambition, confidence, desire and attraction

Capable – see confidence

Captivated – see curiosity

Careful – see apathy and boredom, ambiguity

Caring – see desire and attraction, apathy and boredom

Cautious – see apathy and boredom, jealousy

Centred – see equanimity

Cheating – see betrayal

Clinging – see fear, jealousy

Commiserating – see pity

Compassion – see kindness, love, happiness

Complaining – see bitterness, hurt and heartbreak

Composed – see equanimity

Compulsion – see addiction

Concealment – see betrayal

Condescending – see contempt

Confidence – see acceptance, happiness, equanimity, trust, forgiveness

Confusion and ambiguity – see worthlessness and self-loathing, suspicion, vulnerability

Connected – see love

Considered – see ambiguity, equanimity

Contempt – see hate, greed and possessiveness, envy, jealousy

Contrite – see shame

Controlling – see jealousy

Cool-headed – see equanimity

Courage – see vulnerability, fear, failure, love

Covetous – see ambition

Craving – see desire and attraction, addiction

Creative – see acceptance

Culpable – shame

Cynical – see ambiguity

Deceit – see betrayal

Defeated – see failure

Deferential – see envy

Déjà vu – see regret

Dejected – see disappointment, failure

Delight – see happiness

Depression – see sadness, worry and anxiety, worthlessness and self-loathing

Derision – see disgust, contempt

Desire – see envy, addiction, ambition, love

Desperation – see fear

Despising – see hurt and heartbreak, envy

Despondent – sadness

Detached – see equanimity

Devastated – see betrayal

Devotion – see addiction

Disappointment – see loneliness, worthlessness and self-loathing

Disbelief – see betrayal

Discerning – see contempt

Discombobulated – see desire and attraction

Discontented – see envy

Disgust – see contempt, hate

Disillusioned – see disappointment

Dislike – see disgust, contempt, anger

Dissatisfied – see envy

Distaste – see disgust

Distrustful – jealousy

Double-crossing – see betrayal

Doubtful – see ambiguity

Dread – see ambiguity, fear

Driven – see busyness and haste, ambition

Dubious – see ambiguity

Eager – see ambition

Ecstasy – see happiness

Elation – see happiness

Embarrassed – see shame

Enchanted – see love

Ennui – see apathy and boredom

Enslavement – see addiction

Envy – see jealousy, greed and possessiveness, love

Equanimity and contentment – see love, kindness, shame, vulnerability, worry and anxiety

Exasperated – see anger

Exhaustion – see ambition

Enthusiasm – see ambition

Euphoric – see love, happiness

False – see betrayal

Fascination – see disgust

Fearless – see courage

Fixated – see hate

Flexibility – see acceptance

Flirtatious – see desire and attraction
Forlorn – see regret
Free – see acceptance, envy
Friendly – see curiosity
Frightened – see fear
Frustration – see anger
Furious – see anger, envy

Generous – see kindness
Glee – see happiness
Goal-oriented – see busyness and haste
Go-getting – see ambition
Greed and possessiveness – see ambition,
    envy, jealousy
Grief – see sadness, loneliness, love,
    disappointment
Guilty – see shame, addiction

Happiness – see love, kindness,
    confidence
Harshness – see worthlessness and self-
    loathing, bitterness, anger
Hate – see contempt, envy, disgust
Heroic – see courage
Hesitant – see confidence, ambiguity
Homecoming – see déjà vu, trust
Honour – see courage, grief
Hopeful – see confidence
Hostile – see anger
Humble – see anger, confidence
Hurt – see resentment, bitterness, anger,
    fear, worry and anxiety

Imitating – see envy
Imperturbable – see equanimity
Importance – see busyness and haste
Inactive – see apathy and boredom
Indignant – see anger
Infatuated – see desire and attraction
Inquisitive – see curiosity
Integration – see acceptance
Interested – see curiosity, desire and
    attraction
Interfering – see curiosity
Intimate – see love
Intrigued – see curiosity
Irritated – see anger
Insatiable – see greed and possessiveness

Isolated – see addiction

Jealousy – see bitterness, anger, grief,
    disappointment
Joy – see happiness

Kindness – see love, trust, forgiveness

Let down – see disappointment
Listless – see apathy and boredom
Loathing – see disgust, hate
Loneliness – see sadness, worthlessness
    and self-loathing
Longing – see envy
Lost – see regret
Love – see kindness, trust, desire and
    attraction, addiction
Litigious – see suspicion, resentment
Lustful – see desire and attraction
Lying – see betrayal

Maniacal – see ambition
Meddling – see curiosity
Melancholy and sadness – see worry and
    anxiety, worthlessness and self-loathing,
    shame
Miserable – see sadness
Moral certainty – see contempt
Morose – see sadness
Mysticism – see déjà vu

Needed – see busyness and haste
Nervousness – see fear
Nostalgia and regret – see sadness,
    disappointment
Nosy – see curiosity

Obligated – see kindness
Obsession – see addiction, desire and
    attraction, hate
Open-minded – see ambiguity
Openness – see acceptance
Opting out – see apathy and boredom
Optimistic – see confidence
Overlooked – see envy
Overwhelmed – see busyness and haste

Panic – see fear
Paralysis – see ambiguity

Passionate – see ambition, love, desire and attraction

Perplexed – see déjà vu

Petty – see jealousy

Pity – see kindness, contempt, hate, love, rejection

Playful – see acceptance, desire and attraction

Pleasure – see happiness

Poor self-care – see addiction

Positive – see confidence

Possessive – see jealousy

Prevaricating – see ambiguity

Prickly – angry

Pride – see happiness, envy

Puzzled – see curiosity

Questioning – see ambiguity

Rage – see anger, apathy and boredom

Realistic – see disappointment

Reckless – see confidence

Recrimination – grief, regret

Reflective – see ambiguity

Regret – see anger

Rejection – see hate, contempt, shame, vulnerability

Rejoicing – see happiness

Remorseful – see regret

Removed – see apathy and boredom

Repugnance – see disgust, shame

Repulsion – see disgust

Resentment – see contempt, bitterness, grief

Return – see déjà vu

Revulsion – see disgust

Righteous – see disgust, contempt, anger

Rigid – see disgust

Risky – see courage

Rivalrous – see envy, jealousy

Ruminative – see worry and anxiety, trauma

Sabotage – see betrayal

Scared – see fear, disgust

Sceptical – see ambiguity

Self-compassion – see acceptance, kindness

Self-critical – see confidence, envy

Self-deprecating – see worthlessness and self-loathing, sadness

Self-efficacy – see confidence

Self-worth – see acceptance

Shame – see vulnerability, worry and anxiety, worthlessness and self-loathing

Shocked – see fear

Sickened – see disgust

Solitude – see loneliness

Sorrow – see sadness

Stricken – see sadness, fear

Successful – see ambition, busyness and haste

Suffering – see anger

Sure – see confidence

Seething – see anger

Shamed – see failure

Spiteful – see contempt

Stalking – see desire and attraction

Successful – see ambition

Superiority – see contempt

Surprise – see fear, ambiguity, appreciation, trust

Suspicion – see love, betrayal, jealousy

Thoughtful – see ambiguity

Thrilled – see happiness

Tolerant – see acceptance, ambiguity

Traumatized – see betrayal, fear

Treachery – see betrayal

Trepidation – see fear

Trust – see love, confidence, forgiveness

Type A – see busyness and haste

Uncertain – see ambiguity

Undermining – see betrayal

Understanding – see acceptance, pity

Unfaithful – see betrayal

Vainglory – see ambition and pride

Vengeful – see anger, resentment

Violated – see betrayal

Vulnerable – see courage, hurt and heartbreak, acceptance

Wanted – see busyness and haste, desire and attraction

Index of feelings

Index of physical signs
of feelings

The vast majority of communication between people is physical. It has been estimated that 93 per cent of the information we deliver is non-verbal. The words exchanged are only a small portion (7 per cent) of this.

This index covers the physical signs of feelings. To be more certain that these are signalling the most appropriate underlying feeling, we need to consider:

- the person's usual rate of this physical action
- the context in terms of social situation
- the sequence of actions.

Verbal

Making demeaning or belittling comments – may indicate jealousy or envy

Laughter – may indicate happiness

Higher-pitched laughter – anxiety or fear

Talkative – may indicate happiness

Enthusiastic voice – may indicate happiness

Openness and expansiveness – may indicate happiness and trust

Breathlessness – may indicate sadness or anxiety

Sighing – may indicate sadness, relaxation or relief

Cynical comments – may indicate apathy, insecurity or boredom

Coughing before speaking – may indicate hesitancy, fear, indecision or reluctance

Crying – may indicate sadness or deep love

Head, face, hair and skin

Smiling – may indicate happiness, kindness

Half-smile – summoning patience, tolerating

Fixed smiling – anxiety or fear

Open face – may indicate happiness

Head in hands – may indicate exhaustion

Face flushed or hot – may indicate anger or embarrassment and shame

Face scrunches up – may indicate fear or distress

One side of the face contorts into a smirk or sneer – may indicate contempt

An index finger placed vertically against the cheek bone under the eye – may indicate concern or suspicion

Head stroking – may indicate ambivalence, doubt and indecision

Temples throbbing – may indicate fear

Interlaced fingers behind the head, cobra position – may indicate confidence

Playing with or twisting hair – may indicate apathy or boredom

Playing with hair with palm facing out exposing underside or wrists – may indicate that the person trusts you

Running fingers through hair – may indicate that the person trusts you

Goose bumps – may indicate fear

Mottled upper chest – heightened arousal

Acne – adrenal activity

Bruising, especially of inner arms – possible sign of recent assault

Picking at skin, cuticles or imaginary lint – anxiety

Ventilating hair (lifting hair away from the back of the neck) – may indicate that the person trusts you

Eyes

Eye rubbing – consideration, change of thinking (or exhaustion)

Eye rolling – may indicate apathy or boredom, or contempt

Fixed stare/glare – may indicate anger or jealousy or hate

Looking at the sky – may indicate appreciation

Pupils constrict – may indicate disappointment

Pupils dilate – may indicate happiness or pleasure

Tired-looking eyes – may indicate exhaustion

Tightening of eye focus – may indicate fear

Eye squint – confusion, disagreement

Staring – may indicate fear, contempt

Eyes bulging – may indicate fear or stress

Eyes scanning and darting before intensely focusing – may indicate fear, alertness

Eyes tense – may indicate disappointment

Longer more frequent looks – may indicate attraction and desire

Droopy eyelids – may indicate sadness, weariness

Direct eye contact – may indicate confidence

Forehead, eyebrows and ears

Hands on forehead – dismay

Rubbing temples – concern

Frowning – may indicate anger, disapproval, sadness

Eyebrows arched – may indicate suspicion or surprise

Eyebrows knitted – may indicate anger

Eyebrows raised – may indicate appreciation or surprise

Inner ends of the eyebrows contract in addition to the downturning of the lips – may indicate sadness

Ears flushed – may indicate anger, embarrassment and shame

Rubbing behind ears – anxious, trying to self-soothe

Nose, jaw and chin

Asymmetrical nose wrinkling – may indicate hate

Nostrils flare – may indicate fear and sometimes shock or anger

Tapping nose with index finger – may indication ambivalence, doubt and indecision

Rubbing both sides of nose – concern

Muscles tensing, especially the jaw – may indicate jealousy

Chin quivering – may indicate fear

Jutting jaw – may indicate anger

Chin up – may indicate confidence, contempt or arrogance

Chin cradling – may indicate apathy or boredom, exhaustion

Chin stroking – consideration

Mouth and lips

Lip stroking or plucking – may indication ambition and pride

Thin-lipped – suppression of opinion

Pursed lips – anger

Teeth clenching – may indicate jealousy

Exhalation with lips left slightly open – may indicate disappointment

Clenching teeth – may indicate fear

Teeth baring – may indicate fear

Yawning – may indicate apathy or boredom

Compressed lips – may indicate suspicion

Lips turned downwards – may indicate sadness

Twisting of the lips – may indicate contempt

Smiles less – may indicate confidence

Flicking thumbnail on teeth – may indicate worry

Touching the area between the upper lip and the nose (the philtrum) – may indicate worry

Breathing and heart rate

Choking sensation – may indicate jealousy

Fast heart rate – may indicate jealousy

Holding their breath (in freeze) – may indicate worry

Gasp – shock

Sigh – grief, sadness or soothing before expressing an idea

Neck and shoulders

Rubbing neck – may indicate anxiety

Difficulty swallowing – may indicate sadness

Shrugging – fear or alertness

Shrugging one shoulder – dismissive or deceptive

Turtling – shoulders up, head down – fear

Body and body alignment

Muscles tensing or cramping – may indicate fear

Getting cold and clammy – may indicate fear

Jumping up and down – may indicate happiness

Shoulders widening – may indicate confidence

Standing tall – may indicate confidence

Leans back – may indicate confidence

Leaning in – may indicate interest, desire and appreciation

Faster heart beat – may indicate fear

Shuddering – may indicate sadness

Asymmetrical – pain physical or emotional

Chest, arms and shoulders

Flushed chest – may indicate anxiety, embarrassment, desire

Hand pressed against upper left side of chest – anxiety

Raised arms near but not touching the face – may indicate fear

Shrug of a shoulder – may indicate contempt

Arm spreading – may indicate confidence

One shoulder rises – may indicate desire

Placing a hand against the opposite shoulder and rubbing – may indicate worry

Crossed arms – determination or reassuring self

Hands

Hugging people – may indicate happiness

Too-vigorous handshake – may indicate confidence

Too-vigorous handshake – may indicate anger

Clenching fists – may indicate anger

Hands clasped behind head – confident

Hands clasped behind back – trying to appear to be confident

Fiddling with watch or jewellery – tense

Stomach and intestines

Butterflies in the tummy – may indicate fear

Feeling nauseous – may indicate fear

Gait

Uncoordinated or misaligned – trauma

Legs

Pulled back under seat while
seated – withholding
Leg splayed – may indicate confidence,
possibly domineering over-confidence
Crossed towards someone – closeness,
alignment
Crossed away from someone – may be
seeking distance
Two people with crossed legs
'wagging' – intimacy
Knee hugging – soothing

Thigh rubbing downwards with both
hands – ready to go, determined
Sitting with locked ankles – withholding
Standing with legs crossing at calf level –
confidence, familiarity

Feet

Standing with feet crossed – may indicate
that the person trusts you
Tapping – impatience
Direction of feet often indicates where the
person wants to go

End notes

Page 1   'Our bodies have six main senses: touch, smell, taste, sight, hearing and haptic …' Proffitt, D., and Drake, B. (2020) *Perception: How Our Bodies Shape Our Minds*, St Martin's Press.

Page 3   'Ordinarily we do not discover the wisdom of our feelings …' Watts, A. (2011) *Become What You Are*, Shambhala Pocket Library, Random House.

Page 5   'One of the most perplexing things to realise, as Lisa Feldman Barratt points out is …' Barrett, L. F. (2017). *How Emotions are Made: The Secret Life of the Brain*, Pan Books.

Page 12   'Your body is an intricate information processing system with each part affecting others.' Damasio, A. R. (2005). *Descartes' Error: Emotion, Reason and the Human Brain*, Vintage books.

Page 13   'When I accept myself just as I am, then I can change.' Carl R. Rogers (1995) *On Becoming a Person: A Therapist's View of Psychotherapy*, Mariner Books.

Page 15   'Sigmund Freud called this "projection"… Freud, A. (2018) *Ego and the Mechanisms of Defense*, Routledge.

Page 16   'One way to get through contradictions like this is to complete a process called "inner work" … Johnson, R. (1989) *Inner Work: Using Dreams and Active Imagination for Personal Growth*, Harper Collins.

Page 23   'The greater the doubt …' – C. C. Chang. (1978) *The Practice of Zen*, Greenwood-Heinemann Publishing.

Page 33   'People with tempers and anger issues are at higher risk of heart problems.' Sapolsky, R. (2017) *Behave: The Biology of Humans at our Best and Worst*, Penguin.

Page 38   'As 80 per cent of communication is non-verbal … Mehrabian, A. (2017) *Nonverbal Communication*, Routledge.

Page 44   'Thaddeus Golas, the author of *The Lazy Man's Guide to Enlightenment*, writes …' Golas, T. (1971) *The Lazy Man's Guide to Enlightenment*, Seed Center.

Page 58   'As the Zen teaching Koan instructs: "Hold on tight with an open palm." Loori, D. J. (ed) (2012) *Sitting with Koans: Essential Writings on Zen Koan Introspection*, Wisdom Publications.

Page 59   'Stephen Covey's book *First Things First* contains the wonderful adage that …' Covey, S., Merrill, A. R., and Merill, R. R. (2015) *First Things First*, Franklin Covey.

Page 85   'Rene Girard, the French philosopher, called this "memetic desire". Cayley, D. (Ed.) (2019) *The Ideas of Rene Girard: An Anthropology of Violence and Religion*, David Cayley.

Page 94   'The disgusted brain ...' Sapolsky, R. (2017) *Behave: The Biology of Humans at Our Best and Worst*, Penguin.

Page 94   'People do this based on their perceptions of two personal characteristics ...' Fiske, S., Glick, P., and Xu, J. (2002). 'A model of (often mixed) stereotype content: Competence and warmth respectively follow from perceived status and competition', *Journal of Personality and Social Psychology*, 82, 6, 878–902.

Page 95   '... feel disgusted by them.' Ibid.

Page 99   '... it can make people far less prone to feeling embarrassed.' The work was presented in a talk by Sturm Thursday (14 April) at the 64th annual American Academy of Neurology meeting in Hawaii. https://www.livescience.com/13727-embarrassment-brain-dementia.html

Page 106   'From the writings of the Japanese Priest, Nichiren Daishonin ...' https://www.nichirenlibrary.org/en/wnd-1/Content/95/

Page 113   'In her book *Unchained Memories* psychiatrist and author Lenore Terr ...' Terr, L. (1994) *Unchained Memories: True Stories of Traumatic Memories Lost and Found*, Perseus.

Page 115   'Leonard Cohen took five years to write his now world-famous song 'Hallelujah'. https://www.washingtonpost.com/news/morning-mix/wp/2016/11/11/leonard-cohens-hallelujah-pops-most-sacred-text-almost-went-unheard-by-the-masses/

Page 117   'Fear is like fire. If you can control it, it can cook for you, it can heat your home ...' Ishida, S. (2015) *Tokyo Ghoul*, VIZ Media LLC.

Page 135   'The grieving brain.' https://www.addictionblog.org/recovery/grief-and-addiction-recovery-identifying-existential-grief/

Page 136   'I have reigned more than fifty years in victory and peace ...' Lotus Sutra Lecture, Chapters XXI and XXII (Podcast, 9 May 2019).

Page 137   'After his run Jack was asked about his life ...' https://www.theage.com.au/national/farewell-to-a-gentle-veteran-20020527-gdu8rj.html

Page 144   'As author Robert Sapolsky points out ...' 10 May 2017, https://ideas.ted.com/why-you-want-to-wash-your-hands-when-you-feel-guilty/

Page 162 'You never really understand a person until you consider things from his point of view ...' Lee, H. (2001) *To Kill a Mockingbird*, Random House.

Page 163   'As Quentin Crisp advised: "Neither look forward where there is doubt ..."' https://www.goodreads.com/quotes/397348-neither-look-forward-where-there-is- doubt-nor-backward-where

Page 171   'Oh would I were the sea wind ...' Wright, F. A. (1938). In *The Oxford Book of Greek Verse in Translation* (Eds.) T. T. F. Higham and C. M. Bowra, Oxford.

Page 178   'The loved-up brain.' https://sites.tufts.edu/emotiononthebrain/2014/12/08/the-neuroscience-of-love/

Page 182   'The obsessive brain ...' https://www.calmclinic.com/other/ocd-and-brain

Page 185   'Gordon Livingston has a great term (and a wonderful book) for this: "Too soon old, too late smart". Livingstone, G. (2005) *Too Soon Old, Too Late Smart: Thirty Things You need to Know Now*, Hodder.

Page 200 'There was a contest of wisdom once held in Ancient Greece ...' O'Donohue, J. (2011) *Four Elements: Reflections on Nature*, Harmony.

Page 209   'Being surprised causes humans to physically freeze for 1/25th of a second.' https://www.wnycstudios.org/podcasts/takeaway/segments/surprise-unexpected-why-it-feels-good-and-why-its-good-us

Page 210   'A recent study from the University of California, Berkeley, found that those people who experience more awe in their life ...' Piff, P. K., Dietze, P., Feinberg, M., Stancato, D. M., & Keltner, D. (2015). 'Awe, the small self, and prosocial behavior', *Journal of Personality and Social Psychology*, 108(6), 883–99.

Page 213   'A classic example of suspicion is game theory's exercise called the Prisoner's Dilemma.' Sapolsky, R. (2010) Human Behavioural Biology (lecture).

Page 215   'The suspicious brain.' https://www.sciencedaily.com/releases/2012/05/120517132123.htm

Page 216   'Traumatised people chronically feel unsafe inside their bodies ...' Van der Kolk, B. (2014) *The Body Keeps the Score: Brain, Mind, and Body in the Healing of Trauma*, Penguin House.

Page 232   'To paraphrase the thoughts of Nikos Kazantzakis, what a strange creation humans are ... ' https://quotefancy.com/quote/1047282/Nikos-Kazantzakis-What-a-strange-machine-man-is-You-fill-him-with-bread-wine-fish-and

Page 232   'Of the 11,000,200,000 bits of information that assail or entice our senses every second ...' Norretranders, T. (1999) *The User Illusion: Cutting Consciousness Down to Size*, Penguin.

Page 236   'Young people check their phones on average about 150 times a day ...' https://economictimes.indiatimes.com/tech/hardware/smartphone-users-check-mobiles-150-times-a-day-study/articleshow/18443780.cms?from=mdr

Page 244   'More young women than young men tend to regard themselves as worthless.' Fuller, A. *How to Build Resilience – A study of 290,000 school students*, available from www.andrewfuller.com.au

Page 246   'The self-loathing brain.' https://healthland.time.com/2011/10/04/tracing-circuits-of-self-loathing-in-the-depressed-brain/